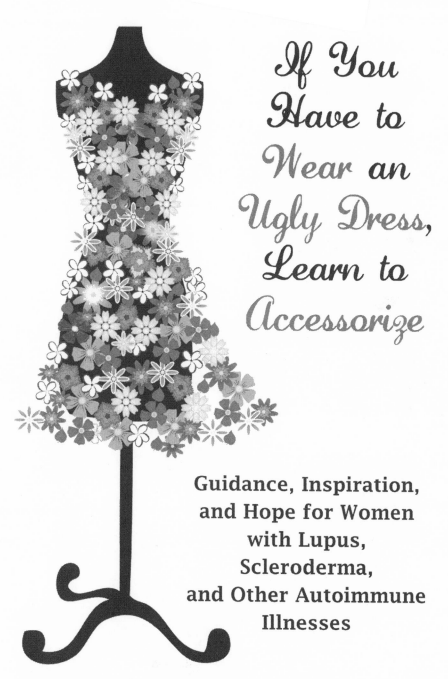

If You Have to Wear an Ugly Dress, Learn to Accessorize

Guidance, Inspiration, and Hope for Women with Lupus, Scleroderma, and Other Autoimmune Illnesses

Linda McNamara, RN, MBA ✽ Karen Kemper, MSPH, PhD

Dedication

In the course of our journeys, we have met so many of you who are living with serious illnesses, yet you wear your ugly dresses with quiet dignity and grace. You have inspired us and have shaped the way we think about our own illnesses.

We hope our book will validate your experiences and suggest ways of reframing your problems to make them more manageable. We hope you will find, as we have, that health is so much more than the absence of disease. Real health encompasses connectedness, peace, joy, healthy relationships, and the ability to survive change.

Contents

Part 1: The Ugly Dress

Part 2: Accessorizing the Ugly Dress

Introduction

Who Are We?

*K*AREN AND I are health professionals who are living healthy, happy, and productive lives in spite of serious autoimmune illnesses—in our cases, lupus and scleroderma. I am a registered nurse, healthcare consultant, and a certified health coach. Because of my experience and interest in improving the health and well-being of others, I have served as a health adviser to many organizations. I served on the Director's Council of Public Representatives for the National Institutes of Health (NIH), the world's premier medical research entity, from 2006 to 2010. Because of the medical research done through the NIH, people are living longer and better. Currently, I am participating in the National Multicultural Outreach Initiative for the National

Institute of Arthritis and Musculoskeletal and Skin Diseases (NIAMS). The mission of NIAMS is to support research into the causes, treatment, and prevention of arthritis and musculoskeletal and skin diseases (including scleroderma, lupus, and rheumatoid arthritis). This includes training scientists and sharing information with the public as they learn more about these diseases. Karen is a health educator with a PhD in public health, health promotion, and is a university professor in public health. She has certifications in health fitness from the American College of Sports Medicine and life coaching from the Life Coaching Institute and has worked in health and wellness for twenty-five years. She serves on the board for the South Carolina Chapter of the Scleroderma Association and assists with their local support group and statewide patient initiatives.

Karen and I met at Clemson University in 1994. I was the director of the Joseph F. Sullivan Center, an academic nurse-managed health center, and she was an assistant professor in the Department of Public Health Sciences. We worked closely together on numerous projects and became friends.

What Is the Ugly Dress?

The "ugly dress" is a metaphor for chronic illness. When I was diagnosed with lupus, Karen had already been living with scleroderma for several years. I admired the way she dealt with her illness with such grace and style. I asked her one day how she did it. She told me that when she was diagnosed with scleroderma, she wrote a poem describing her illness as an ugly dress. She said that she didn't want to wear an ugly dress, but it was handed to her and she had no other option. The ugly dress was simply a fact of life.

I replied, "Karen, you know what I do when I have to wear an ugly dress? I accessorize!" Thus began the concept for this book. Karen and I decided to consciously and carefully select "accessories" to overcome the "ugly" of our illnesses and to enhance the quality of our lives.

What Are "Accessories"?

Our accessories are the attitudes, beliefs, and behaviors we've embraced to remake our ugly dresses of scleroderma and lupus. We acknowledge that the ugly dresses of lupus, scleroderma, and other serious illnesses will never be beautiful. As my grandmother always said, "You can't make a silk purse from a sow's ear." Chronic illness is what it is. When you live with it on a daily basis, you have to deal with lots of ugliness including fear, anger, pain, and fatigue. By carefully choosing accessories, Karen and I have found ways to manage our illnesses so that our ugly dresses don't keep us from living happy and productive lives.

Why Did We Write This Book?

Because of the horrendous impact scleroderma and lupus have had on our lives, we decided to write this book to offer hope and encouragement to others. Rachel Naomi Remen, MD, said in *Kitchen Table Wisdom*, "Expertise cures, but wounded people can best be healed by other wounded people. Only other wounded people can understand what is needed, for the healing of suffering is compassion, not expertise." Over the past sixteen years, Karen and I have shared fears and frustrations about our illnesses as well as coping strategies and dreams for the future. We've each struggled through overwhelming feelings of loss, grief, anger, fear, and powerlessness. We've navigated a health-care system filled with individuals who are often patronizing and sometimes dismissive. We've fielded well-intentioned but hurtful remarks such as, "But you look so good," the implied meaning seeming to be, "You can't possibly be sick." We've overcome pain, extreme fatigue, and mental cloudiness in order to continue working. We've walked the tightrope between seeking and accepting help and fiercely guarding our independence. This book describes our personal journeys. We've both moved from a narrow focus on physical health and disease management to a new and broader understanding of health, well-being, and fruitful living. Just as life is not a straight path but is filled with disruptions and chaos, so were our journeys. We use a collection of personal stories, anecdotes, and poetry to describe our experiences. The purpose of our book is threefold: to validate the overwhelming feelings associated with having a chronic illness, to offer insight and inspiration through personal examples and poetry, and to provide strategies for achieving health and well-being in spite of illness.

A Disclaimer

Although our book is sometimes lighthearted in approach, we acknowledge the very real suffering of people with serious illnesses. We have found humor to be a very useful tool to help us cope, but it is never our intent to in any way trivialize the pain and suffering of others.

Who Is the Intended Reader?

Our book is written directly to and for women who are living with lupus, scleroderma, or other autoimmune illnesses. However, the concepts can benefit everyone experiencing a long-term illness or disability—as well as their friends and family.

How Is the Book Organized?

In the first part of the book, we talk about autoimmune illnesses in general and lupus and scleroderma specifically. We describe what it is like to wear our ugly dresses of scleroderma and lupus. In the second part, we discuss how we use the accessories of helpful attitudes, beliefs, and behaviors on a daily basis to help us manage not only our illnesses but our lives. We describe specific strategies we use to manage feelings and time and energy, and to navigate the health-care system, manage perceptions, and achieve overall health and well-being. In the Afterword, we describe how our lives have changed because of our ugly dresses.

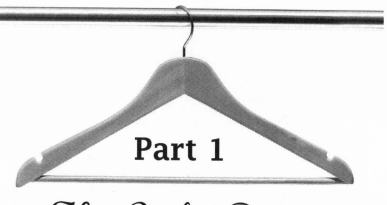

Part 1

The Ugly Dress

About Autoimmune Illnesses

$\mathcal{I}$N ALL AUTOIMMUNE illnesses, the underlying problem is similar—the body's immune system cannot distinguish between "self" and "non-self" and produces antibodies against the body's own cells (auto-antibodies), causing inflammation and tissue damage. The specific symptoms of an autoimmune disease depend on which tissues or organs are targeted. For example, if the skin is targeted there may be rashes, blisters, or color changes. If the kidneys are targeted, there can be kidney failure.

The body's immune system is designed to protect the body from foreign invaders such as viruses and other infectious organisms. To put it in nonmedical language, imagine the average person's immune system as a well-trained, disciplined army. This highly trained army is on alert at all times for invasion by a virus, bacteria, cancer cell, etc. When an invasion occurs, the specialists in the body's army go to work doing their specific jobs and the invasion is usually handled efficiently and effectively. The body has been protected. The army has done its job and "stands down." Now imagine the army of the person with an autoimmune illness. The army is untrained, undisciplined, and can't distinguish a true invader from the body's own tissues. Chaos ensues, thus damaging the very body the army is designed to protect.

According to the American Autoimmune-Related Diseases Association there are currently 149 unique autoimmune or autoimmune-related diseases. Of the fifty million Americans living with autoimmune diseases, more than 75 percent are women. Autoimmune disease is one of the top ten leading causes of death in women under sixty-five. Some of the major autoimmune diseases include scleroderma, lupus, Crohn's disease, ulcerative colitis, type-1 diabetes, multiple sclerosis, rheumatoid arthritis, and psoriasis.

Scleroderma

Educational materials about scleroderma most commonly start with the medical translation of the term scler/o/derma, which literally means "hard skin" in Greek. Scleroderma is an autoimmune disease that is characterized by changes in connective tissue that result in loss of function and potential system failure of several organs of the body. Changes to the skin, hands, and face are the most apparent external changes that often define scleroderma, but it is actually the damage within the body that proves to be the real threat. It is believed that some trigger or glitch in the immune system results in the body attacking itself and setting off a chain reaction of inflammation and overproduction of collagen in certain tissues. The excess collagen changes how the tissue functions, to some extent choking off oxygen and other nutrients to various parts of the body and trapping the tissue within its own web of protein.

The cause of scleroderma is unknown, but it is thought that people who develop it might have some type of genetic vulnerability to rheumatic disease, which is triggered by some factor from their external environment (for example, pollutants or viruses) or internal environment (such as stress-related chemistry or oxygen stresses). We will probably find that multiple scenarios could ultimately cause the immune changes that result in scleroderma.

We have no epidemiological studies to provide us with accounts of how many and what types of people get scleroderma or what their long-term outcome is. It is considered a rare disease, affecting an estimated 300,000 people in the United States. It is found more often in women than men, though men who have it often have a poorer outcome than women. Long-term outcomes are quite variable and some people live many decades with scleroderma. There appears to be a window of time within the first five years after diagnosis that plays an important role in predicting how rapidly or aggressively the disease might progress. If an individual does not have severe organ damage within the first five years, their long-term outcome is likely to be more favorable. Of course, these are only educated guesses and there is still a lot to learn about managing and treating scleroderma.

There are two main types of scleroderma, each of which has two subtypes. Each type varies in severity and the way it affects the body: localized scleroderma (morphea and localized) and systemic scleroderma (limited and diffuse). Localized scleroderma commonly affects a local area of skin and is more likely to occur in children. It is considered the least life threatening though it can create considerable discomfort to the individual, depending on the location of the affected skin. Systemic scleroderma affects the internal organs as well as external appearance and is more likely to occur in adults. It also may pose a greater risk to the individual's functioning and longevity. Diffuse systemic scleroderma is typically considered the most severe. It has the greatest potential for affecting critical organs and thereby increases the risk of serious organ debilitation or premature death.

Some of the common features of systemic scleroderma are:

- tight, thickened skin on the hands, face, arms, and legs
- compromised circulation, particularly in the hands (Raynaud's phenomenon) and intolerance of cold
- digital (finger) ulcers
- loss of digits (fingers) or contracted fingers
- swelling in hands and feet
- compromised gastrointestinal functioning, accompanied by chronic reflux
- narrowing of the opening of the mouth and diminished oral health
- diminished lung function (a leading cause of death in scleroderma)
- compromised heart and kidney function

Currently, no cure exists for scleroderma. However, several treatment options are available that aid in the management of symptoms and slowing of the damage caused by the immune system. Many treatment advances have been made that have improved quality of life and longevity for people with scleroderma. Treatments for reflux, pulmonary hypertension, kidney disease, and Raynaud's phenomenon are some of the most common and successful treatments available. For more information about the types of scleroderma, symptoms, and treatments go to the Scleroderma Foundation website at http://www.scleroderma.org/.

Lupus

There are several types of lupus but systemic lupus erythematosis (SLE) is what most people refer to when they talk about lupus. Systemic means that the disease can affect any part of the body. Discoid lupus is a skin disorder with a red, raised rash on the face, scalp, or elsewhere on the body. The lesions may cause scarring. Some with discoid lupus may later develop SLE. Drug-induced lupus is a form of lupus caused by certain medications. The symptoms are similar to SLE but typically they go away when the drug is stopped. Neonatal lupus can occur in a newborn of women with SLE; however, this is rare.

At present there is no cure for lupus but there is hope. Thirty years ago when people were diagnosed with lupus, they faced the chance of dying within five years. Today because of treatment advances such as the wider use of antimalarial drugs, more conservative use of steroids, and the use of aspirin or anticoagulants for lupus patients with clotting abnormalities, lupus patients can enjoy a longer life span and better quality of life.

The cause of lupus is still unknown. A number of genes have been associated with lupus risk. So if you have a certain gene or combination of genes, you might be at higher risk for the disease but you won't develop it until something in the environment turns on your immune system. Some environmental triggers may include sun exposure, viruses and other infectious agents, and certain drugs. The Epstein-Barr virus (EBV), the same virus that causes mononucleosis, may be related to the development of lupus in some people.

Ninety percent of lupus patients are female. The disease is three to four times more common in African Americans than in Caucasians. It is also more common in Hispanics, Asians, and Native Americans.

Symptoms of lupus range from mild to very serious and life threatening. Major organ damage is possible for many. There are numerous symptoms of lupus depending on the tissues or organs involved, but two of the most common are joint and muscle aches and pains and disabling fatigue. Other symptoms are skin rashes, photosensitivity, unexplained fevers, sores or ulcers in mouth or nose, enlarged lymph nodes, hair loss, nephritis (inflammation of the kidneys), pleuritis (inflammation of sac surrounding the lungs), and pericarditis (inflammation around the heart). If the lupus affects the brain or central nervous system, headaches, dizziness, memory problems, vision problems, seizures, stroke, or changes in behavior may occur. Patients with lupus are also at increased risk of atherosclerosis (hardening of the blood vessels that can cause heart attack or stroke).

Symptoms may come and go with periods of increased

activity, called flares, and periods of inactivity, called quiet periods. One of the keys to managing lupus is to recognize the warning signs of a flare in order to take steps to prevent the flare or decrease the impact. You can find reliable information about lupus at the Lupus Foundation of America website (http://www.lupus.org) or the National Library of Medicine Medline Plus website (http://nlm.nih.gov/medlineplus).

Karen's Ugly Dress ✤Scleroderma

No one knows what causes scleroderma, and I certainly don't know what caused the development of mine, but I feel strongly that it emerged in part because of several life stresses and genetic vulnerability. I have at least four first cousins and one uncle who developed various autoimmune diseases by early adulthood, and while it is not proof of a genetic vulnerability, it does suggest the possibility of one. While the role of genetics is important, I feel that it is the accumulation of life stress that played the greatest role in the development of my scleroderma.

In 1992, I was working on the last stages of my PhD in public health. The work was going well but it was stressful. My personal life had gone through an upheaval but it seemed to be improving. I had a job and a new life in a new town waiting for me.

Then things started to unravel. I was diagnosed with some precancerous cervical cells, my boyfriend decided to reconcile with his old girlfriend, I had to postpone my dissertation defense because of my medical problems, and I was having difficulty sleeping because of relentless worrying. And then there were those pesky symptoms that began during the last months of graduate school. My fingers and hands had become swollen. A small sore had formed on one of my fingertips. Every morning I woke up with a surge in body temperature and a breaking sweat. In hindsight those symptoms were obviously the first stages of scleroderma, but at the time they seemed annoying but not alarming.

About a year before I was diagnosed with scleroderma, there was a short period of time during which the skin on my arms and legs felt itchy right after showering. I had never felt an irritation like this before and attributed it to a reaction to soap. Itchy skin is a miserable symptom of scleroderma that many people experience chronically. Fortunately, this symptom did not last long.

A few months after the itchy skin, I went on a two-day backpacking hike during which I bathed in a very cold mountain stream. My hands turned a translucent white and I lost feeling in several fingers of both hands. It took about thirty minutes for my feeling and color to return. Although it was uncomfortable, I didn't think much of it. My finger-nails and toenails often became blue in cold weather and my feet would sometimes become numb in the winter. Within a month of that incident, however, my fingers started to swell overnight. At first I blamed it on the South Carolina summer heat and sitting at the computer, but it seemed to get pro-gressively worse. Eventually, I couldn't wear my rings and my hands felt inflexible and heavy. Then my feet started to swell. It became difficult to walk in my shoes, and eventu-ally I had to give away all the shoes I had during that time. I bought new shoes that were at least one size bigger than I had worn the previous month. The swelling in my feet would get so bad that I would have blood in my socks after running because my toenails were compressed into my skin.

The symptom that put me over the edge, though, was the finger ulcer. It started out very small. I didn't know how I acquired the ulcer, I didn't remember hurting myself, but there it was. And it wouldn't heal. It was this ulcer that would force me to finally see a doctor. I say *force* because none of the symptoms by themselves seemed serious. I thought they would go away. When they didn't go away, I became worried that if I did have a serious problem and saw a doctor before I started my new job; I might not be able to get health care coverage. I delayed seeking medical care because I feared being labeled with a pre-existing condition. I have been an emotional hostage to health insurance ever since.

When my symptoms of scleroderma first started, I had never heard the word "scleroderma." I just knew that something was wrong with my body. My hands were swelling every day. I kept a record of what was happening so I would remember details that might be important clues if I decided to go to a doctor. The symptoms were a nuisance, but I had so many other things going on in my life that I couldn't give them much attention.

After about a month at my new job, my symptoms had become progressively worse, and I finally decided I needed to see a doctor. I went to a primary care physician recommended by a friend. I explained my symptoms: swollen hands and feet and a sore on my finger that wouldn't heal. I told the doctor that I had been under a lot of stress recently with school, moving, and starting a new job. I was not sure if these symptoms were even linked, but I wanted to share all of the information I could that might help find an answer.

The physician took a cursory look at me and told me that I should come back in six weeks for a complete physical. He said that he didn't think all of these symptoms were necessarily linked and that we would probably never know why my hands were swollen. "And besides," he told me, "this is really just a vanity problem." His words still ring in my ears. When I first heard his comment, I was embarrassed, stunned, and confused. Over time his words would enrage me. This was my introduction to a dark and demoralizing side that the doctor-patient relationship could take.

Within three weeks of the visit with the first physician, the sore on my finger had become so painful that I could not sleep. (I'm glad I didn't know then that every year of my life from that point forward would have at least a dozen pain-filled, sleepless nights like this.) I knew something was wrong but I did not know what to do. The pain was becoming unbearable, but in my gut I knew it was a waste of time and money to go back to the first physician. I had to find someone else.

I asked several friends for recommendations and finally called a second physician's office. I was given an appointment that day. The physician's nurse looked at my finger with thinly veiled horror and the doctor told me, "We are going to try to save your finger." *Try to save my finger?* I couldn't believe what I was hearing. How did I go from "It's just a vanity problem" to "We are going to try to save your finger" in three weeks? The first physician did not tell me that I should care for this sore in any specific way. He did not indicate that there was a risk for such a dangerous infection. But here I was. I was frightened. And I was angry. I did what the new physician said to do and I prayed. Fortunately, the sore improved and I got to keep my finger—or at least most of it.

The second doctor diagnosed me with severe Raynaud's. It was thought to be the cause of my sore but probably not the cause of the swelling. We tried diuretics for the swelling but the swelling did not change. I had heard of Raynaud's in stress management courses and decided to research it. I learned that Raynaud's is often associated with two separate diseases: lupus and scleroderma. I read the description about lupus and did not feel that it described my situation. When I read the description about scleroderma, however, I felt like I was looking in the mirror: sausage-shaped swollen fingers, presence of a positive anti-nuclear antibody, Raynaud's phenomenon with associated ulcers. The only thing I was missing was the hard skin.

I asked a friend who was a medical student at the time about what I had read. He said that I could not diagnose myself. I told him to pull out his textbooks, look up scleroderma, and tell me that the pieces didn't fit. He read the texts and agreed that what we knew so far about my symptoms did suggest that I might be developing scleroderma. I took this information back to the second physician. He also resisted my suggestion that I had scleroderma and pointed out the absence of skin changes. This physician, however, was considerate, compassionate, and supportive. While he was not ready to diagnose me with scleroderma, he did not discount me. I will always appreciate and respect him for that compassion.

By some stroke of wonderful good fortune, one of my former dissertation committee members had heard about my health situation and told me that he was working with an internationally-known researcher at the Medical University of South Carolina (MUSC) who studied Raynaud's. He called her for me and she generously agreed to see me in her lab in Charleston. She examined my hands, looked at my nail beds under a microscope, and told me that I did in fact have more than Raynaud's. She set up an appointment for me to see a rheumatology group at MUSC that specialized in scleroderma. I was assigned to a young woman who was a fellow in the rheumatology group who has been my physician ever since. She has been a patient, calm, and compassionate health care partner for me.

So, by the grace of God, within a year of my first recognizable signs and symptoms, I had an answer for what was wrong with me. Scleroderma. An ugly name for an ugly disease. That diagnosis was the beginning of the end of my view of my future as I had imagined it at thirty years of age. It put me on a different path. Though I don't feel bitter, I still wonder to this day what my life might have looked like without scleroderma.

At some point, though, you have to decide how you will go forward. I decided early on that I wasn't going to have scleroderma and a bad attitude, too. I believe I owe a lot of this outlook to my Aunt Barbara. Barb is my mother's twin sister who was in a serious accident when she was an eighteen-year-old new recruit in the army. She lost her leg in a tragic car accident and was left to rebuild her life and find her way at a time when there were few opportunities for women, let alone disabled women. Barb is a fighter and she has fought for her independence and autonomy her entire life. She never seemed to let her disability stop her from doing what she wanted to do. Yet she has had an ugly dress nonetheless. She lives with pain, physical challenges, and barriers to overcome every day. In spite of these challenges, she is a generous, happy, and caring person with loving family and friends who she has fun with all the time. I am very thankful to her for showing me that you can have a happy, fulfilling life even if things didn't work out the way you thought they would.

My journey with this book started when I began my "relationship" with scleroderma in 1992. Though I had not yet given scleroderma the name "ugly dress," I had to confront my fears about what would come with this disease once I read the word scleroderma. I saw the word for the first time in a medical textbook, and beside it was a photograph of a woman with the disease. The photo was just a small, black-and-white headshot, but when I saw it, I saw into my future. It looked ugly and I believed that I would be ugly, too.

Immediately my brain raced through the consequences of the changes that were going to happen to me. It felt like my life as I knew it was over. I felt fear and anger at being thrown onto this path. I wondered how I would eat, talk, or go out into the world so disfigured. How would it feel to endure the stares and judgments? How would it feel to no longer be me? Who would look back at me in the mirror?

We live in a society where physical appearance, worthiness, and lovability are interrelated. Even if I didn't agree with it, it was an echo I couldn't silence easily. My female identity was linked to my appearance. I never thought of myself as beautiful. I never worked that hard at trying to be beautiful. But I had always felt that my appearance was normal. Now, I would no longer be normal. I would never know my genetically-determined normal aging face. I would have to learn to face the inevitable changes.

The first time someone commented publicly about the changes in my face was at a professional conference. I ran into a fellow student from graduate school. She had not seen me for several years, and she offhandedly commented that I looked "different." She said something about my face (as she gestured around her mouth) looked different, but she didn't know what it was. She didn't say it was good or bad, and she was not being unkind. She was genuinely puzzled. But the comment hit me like a punch in the stomach. It was a reminder that while the physical changes were slow and on a day-to-day basis I didn't notice them ... the changes were happening. And at that moment, I was wearing the ugly dress.

When I was first diagnosed with scleroderma, I didn't really have to wear the dress out in the world. It was only something I experienced in my mind, but other people really couldn't see it. I still don't "wear the dress" all the time. But increasingly, at least once a day, I feel it—when I look in the mirror, use my hands to button a shirt, walk to my office in the cold, try to sleep through the pain of an ulcer, collapse in fatigue at the end of a work day, go to the doctor or dentist, or eat a meal.

Yet there are as many times that I don't have to wear it— when I am laughing with friends, reading a book, walking in summer, listening to music, cuddling the dog, paddling in the kayak. I feel a sense of victory when other people don't see my ugly dress. I feel like I'm holding onto a little of who I was before scleroderma. But the fact is that though I don't "look sick," I have been changed and damaged by scleroderma.

Something I find interesting about my relationship with my ugly dress is that I tend to hide it from my friends and family. I don't want them to see all of it or see the burden it places on me. I don't want to be defined by it. I would rather laugh about it with them. I don't know if this is good or bad, but it is one of the ways that I cope. My family and close friends seem to understand this about me. They are very loving, supportive, and protective, but they don't treat me like a helpless person. They know I am not helpless.

But scleroderma has humbled me, and there are times when facing my limitations has caused a helpless feeling within me. I have become better at asking for help, but living alone means there is usually no one to ask for help for everyday tasks that have become difficult or impossible to do. With my dog as my only witness, I have burst into tears of frustration when I found I could not do a simple task. Once I got so frustrated when I couldn't open a glass jar for a meal I was preparing that I got in my car with the jar and drove down my street looking for help. I stopped my car when I spotted the first man walking in my neighborhood. I got out of the car with my jar and asked if he would open it for me. He did, we both had a good laugh, and I went back home to get back to making dinner.

New relationships can be a challenge when you have an ugly dress, particularly dating relationships. It was harder in the early years of scleroderma because I was still figuring out how I felt about it, so I wasn't sure how to reveal this part of me. I wasn't sure if I should just blurt out "I have an ugly dress called scleroderma!" or if I should keep it to myself. I prefer to have a few conversations with people before I talk about scleroderma to avoid being defined as a person with a disease. After nineteen-plus years, it has become easier to manage the process of sharing this part of my life. I take my time and try to get a sense of the other person's nature as I decide if or when it is necessary for me to discuss sclero- derma. I am never embarrassed to talk about it. As a health educator, I feel that talking about scleroderma can raise awareness about the disease and perhaps help someone else dealing with physical disease.

What I have learned over time is that wearing the ugly dress is about more than the changes to my outer appearance. It is also about the pain, the fatigue, and the uncertainty of what is happening inside my body. What suffering will the ugly dress bring me in the future? These aspects of the ugly dress have turned out to be more important than the disfigurements. I don't like the changes in my face and hands, but for the most part I get used to them and find they don't really matter. What is more challenging to deal with is the suffering that might lie ahead, as well as the fear and frustration that might come with it.

My friends and coworkers typically see me at my highest levels of energy. They don't see me at my low points. I don't hide this part to be heroic. I do it because I don't want to "be" the dress. I don't want to "be" a sick person. I am not scleroderma. I manage scleroderma. It is my shadow but it is not me. I might have to wear the ugly dress, but I do not have to be the ugly dress.

The Ugly Dress

By Karen

Every day, I must open my closet door and look inside.
And there it is, my ugly dress;
Pushed into the back where it can hide.
Sometimes, I try on the ugly dress and see how it feels;
How it looks; how I feel in it.
But I haven't had to wear it out yet.
I still get to take it off and close the door and forget about it.
I know that one day I might not be
able to take off the ugly dress.
And then, I will have to face the whole world
in it . . . when I'd rather be hidden.

The Ugly Dress, Again

By Karen

I have an ugly dress;
It's tight and resists my body's movement.
It makes my skin feel tingly and prickly.
When I move, it feels as though the fabric will tear.
I face the world in this ugly dress.
And its colors are peculiar; mottled with
shades of brown from the sun;
And sprinkled with flecks of white from nicks and scratches.
In my ugly dress, I am an ugly woman.
It blankets my femininity and smothers my youth.
It constricts my essence a little more each day;
Making my breath shudder and my skin
as hard as a warrior's armor.

Face

By Karen

Displaced, Misplaced, Replaced Face.
Reshaped, Disgraced, Misshaped Face.
Distaste, In Haste, Faded Face.
Worst Case, Big Waste, Jaded Face.
Mistake, Too Late, Hated Face.
Wake Up, Make Up, Forsaken Face.

Quiet

By Karen

Quiet. Quiet.
Or you'll miss it fading away,
The draining away of remnants of what might have been.
And I think I'm supposed to be sad today,
'Cause my mind is quietly putting away
The dollies, and trucks, and childhood play
of the one who might have been.

Linda's Ugly Dress ❋ Systemic Lupus

I can trace the start of lupus to 1991, at least five years before I was finally diagnosed. I had excessive tearing in my right eye and was diagnosed with a tear duct obstruction. Despite irrigations of the tear duct, the problem continued. I noticed that the tears always left a grainy residue on my face and that every time I had the grainy discharge from my eye, I felt bad all over. I wondered how something as benign as an obstructed tear duct could make me feel so old and awful.

I finally had surgery to repair the tear duct obstruction in 1992 and hoped the problem was solved. It wasn't. The eye continued with excessive tearing and grainy discharge so I went to another ophthalmologist for a second opinion. The tear duct was open, but the doctor tested both eyes for dryness and said they were both extremely dry. He prescribed lubricating drops and casually asked if I had ever been told I might have an autoimmune disease. No one had ever suggested that before so I didn't think too much about it.

Along with the continuing eye problem, I had recurrent episodes of extreme fatigue, chills, and sore throat. I also had pain in my flanks, muscles, and joints as well as other symptoms. I was in a high-pressure job at the time and working very long hours. I assumed I was just overworked and thus very susceptible to viruses or bacterial infections. Each episode lasted several weeks or sometimes several months. Just when I thought I'd surely die without even knowing what was wrong, I'd get up one day and feel normal again. Then, I'd start the mind game … maybe I really hadn't been that sick. Maybe it was just in my mind. I'd believe that lie until the next time.

I also noticed a decline in my ability to process thoughts. I had always been a quick thinker and very articulate, but there were times since I'd started having the other symptoms when I couldn't think clearly and I had trouble doing relatively simple things such as writing a memo. This frightened me more than any of the other symptoms because my job as a corporate personnel manager depended on my mental abilities. Was I going crazy? Was my estrogen level too low? Was I depressed?

Why did I feel so normal for long periods of time and then so sick? I went to various specialists trying to find an answer. Each looked at my problem through the lens of his or her specialty, but no one looked at the whole picture.

I went to a gastroenterologist because of abdominal swelling and mucous in my stools. He said the symptoms were related to my healthy diet and that I should just cut back on the fiber a bit and see if the symptoms improved. As a nurse with a special interest in wellness, I had always eaten a healthy diet with high fiber, but I only experienced the episodes of swelling and mucous in conjunction with other symptoms such as extreme fatigue and pain in my muscles and joints.

I went to an allergist because I thought allergies might be the cause of the recurrent illnesses. The allergist did a slew of tests and concluded that I wasn't allergic to any of the usual things but might have "chemical sensitivities." I was told to avoid harsh chemicals. Someone told me later that telling someone they have chemical allergies is just a way of dismissing you and your complaints instead of saying directly, "I can't find out what's wrong so you must not be sick."

I had a hysterectomy in 1993, and I actually felt better for a while after the surgery so thought I might have solved the problem. Not so! In retrospect, the feeling better was probably related to the imposed rest period—no work for eight weeks. The symptoms recurred when I started back to work, so I went back to my gynecologist and threatened to stay there until he gave me hormones for what I assumed had to be surgical menopause.

In May 1996, I visited my mother and sisters in Alabama. It was a happy time for me because it was the first time all five sisters had been together since my dad died ten years earlier. My mother was a chain smoker but knowing my sensitivity to smoke, she always refrained from smoking in the house for about a week before I arrived and didn't smoke in the house while I was present. However, her home contained years of smoke residue. My younger sister cleaned heavily before I arrived. She opened all windows to air out the house and used a strong cleaning agent on walls and every surface possible, trying to remove the smoke smell and chemicals. She even bought a new mattress cover and pillows for the guest room. However, after about four days in Mother's home, I began to feel sick (nauseated, tired, achy).

When I returned to South Carolina and to work, I got sicker and sicker. My right eye was again tearing excessively and leaving a granular discharge. The fatigue was overwhelming. I also had severe pain in my back over the left kidney area as well as a low-grade fever. I wondered if I might have a kidney infection. At that time, I was director of a nurse-managed health center at Clemson University, so I asked one of the nurse practitioners to check my urine. She said there was no sign of infection but lots of blood.

I thought back over all the recurrent episodes of illness and recognized a pattern. I told my nurse practitioner that I thought I might have lupus. I called my family doctor and asked to see him that day. I told him that I was not seeing him because of the blood in the urine or the fever but because of the patchwork of symptoms that had recurred over the years and seemed to be getting worse. He did numerous tests to rule out rheumatoid arthritis, lupus, and other illnesses.

He called about a week later to tell me that my antinuclear antibody test was strongly positive and he referred me to a rheumatologist. So I was finally diagnosed with systemic lupus in 1996, five years after the initial symptoms. This is very typical with autoimmune illnesses because the symptoms are often vague and affect different body systems.

I was terrified when I got the diagnosis of lupus because as a nurse, I had seen the terrible effects of this disease. But I was also relieved to finally have a name for the sickness I was feeling. I hate to admit it, but I felt validated. I wanted to say to my husband and others, "See, I told you something was terribly wrong and you would not believe me."

I had started to think that I'd have to die and have an autopsy before anyone discovered what was wrong with me. I knew lots of people, including my husband at the time, thought I was just exaggerating my symptoms and the sickness was all in my head. After all, I didn't look sick! There were no outward signs of my illness, and to the world I looked healthy.

I made up my mind that I would not whine and I would

not be negative. Instead, I vowed to deal with the lupus in a positive way. People all around me were dealing with all kinds of illnesses and other issues, so why should I be exempt? I decided to learn to be as healthy as possible within the constraints of the lupus. Not as easy as it sounds!

Even though I now had a diagnosis, my husband of twenty-eight years was still not convinced I was sick. He believed that I could be well if I just wanted to be, if I just tried harder, exercised more, ate better, and developed a better attitude. He viewed my illness as a contrivance to manipulate and control him.

I tried to be patient with him. After all, I had lived with the symptoms of lupus for years even though I didn't know what was wrong, so I thought it only fair to give him time to adjust. My doctor offered to talk to him, but he refused. I gave him materials to read, which he pointedly ignored. He urged me to see a psychiatrist and check myself into the local mental hospital. He said, "You're just like your mother. You always see the glass half empty while I see the glass half full." He thought that if I could "get fixed mentally," everything would be okay. He brought me books and articles to prove to me that the illness was all in my head and that I chose to be sick and to stay sick.

I am a strong proponent of the mind-body connection, and I know that thoughts affect our physical health, but I also know that there are genetic and biological aspects that one can't control even with positive thinking. His actions reminded me that most of us prefer to have the facts fit our preconceptions. When they don't, it is easier to ignore the facts than to change the preconceptions. My husband refused to learn the facts about lupus because he did not want to let go of his preconceptions.

In January 1997, my precious sister Vickie died unexpectedly at age forty-seven. Grief consumed me. The physical and emotional agony of the grief was overwhelming. I was still working full-time as a director at Clemson University, but the fatigue and other symptoms of the lupus made it difficult to accomplish much. By the time I drove to work, I was already too fatigued to think, and the pain and grief were constant distractions.

One afternoon in May, I felt so fatigued I could hardly move. Pain in my left kidney area was excruciating, and the pain was spreading throughout my body. I had a low-grade temperature. I called my doctor and he increased my prednisone dosage. I began to feel better within a few hours, but the next morning I woke with a temperature of 104 degrees; severe back, muscle, and joint pain; and fatigue such that I was almost catatonic. Later that day, I was hospitalized to rule out infection (none found) and then treated with high-dose intravenous steroids for the lupus.

I experienced all kinds of emotions while alone in my hospital bed, including disbelief that the lupus had made me so sick. I had thought I'd be able to manage the illness by doing all the right things—diet, exercise, rest, pacing myself, and so on. I felt my body had betrayed me, and I felt very alone and vulnerable.

Fear was something I kept pushing back, but it was there as well. That night, when the chest and back pain returned despite the intravenous steroids, I got really scared. I wanted someone with me but told myself I was being selfish and melodramatic.

I knew that if I called, my husband would come back to the hospital, but I also knew that he wouldn't want to be there. I felt so isolated from him. He seemed so cold, so judging, so withdrawn! He was polite and courteous and did and said all the right things, but I realized that he had mentally checked out of our marriage. It was as if the husband I had known and loved had moved behind a steel wall, locked all doors, and was no longer reachable. He did kind things like bring my favorite gown and bedroom shoes to the hospital and arrange for a maid service when I returned home—the kind of things you'd do for an elderly aunt. But he was just a polite and empty shell of my husband.

My doctor again offered to talk to him. Again he refused. When I returned home from the hospital, he had moved out of our bedroom and into the guest room. He said it was for my physical comfort but I wasn't fooled. He was punishing me for being sick and inconveniencing him.

He had always been concerned about my looks, often critical of the way I dressed or concerned that I might be "putting on a little weight." He wanted an attractive, thin, healthy person who would reflect well on him. A sick wife whose appearance was already changing from the high doses of steroids was not who he wanted. He kept moving further and further away emotionally, and I became more and more anxious about our marriage. I tried to talk to him about what was happening but he refused.

One day when I came home from work, he said he'd called a counselor and made an appointment for us. I thought that was a very positive thing to do and said so. After all, we were dealing with other issues in addition to my illness: my sister's death, his father's death in 1995, and his mother's terminal illness. Hopefully, a counselor could help us cope and learn how to keep our marriage together.

I realized later that Mike never believed he needed help. From his perspective, he was doing just fine. He called the counselor hoping she could "fix" me. The counselor told me that he had painted a picture of a pitiful, sick, manipulative woman and told her he feared that I was willing to die from the lupus just to control him. She said she was taken aback when we arrived for the first appointment because she saw an attractive, self-assured woman who was not at all the person she'd imagined from Mike's description. She looked at me, looked at Mike, and said, "I'm confused. Who is the patient? Is it you, Linda? Is it you, Mike? Or is it the marriage?"

Mike said nothing so I naively said, "Well, I think it's all of the above." I explained about the losses and my illness and said that I thought all these things were affecting our marriage.

Mike said, "This is not about me."

When the counselor suggested we assume the marriage was the problem and asked if it was just sick or on life support, Mike said, "It's on life support!" I knew then that the marriage was over in Mike's mind.

He asked for a divorce a few weeks later and I agreed. I simply had no energy to fight for a marriage he no longer wanted. I read once that people love the way they're capable of loving—even if that's not always how you want them to love or how you think they should love. Mike, at that point, was incapable of loving me the way I needed, and likewise, I couldn't love him the way he needed. All my energy had to be spent dealing with the lupus.

So, in less than one year, I lost my sister, my husband, my home, and all sense of security and rightness in my world. Battered, bruised, and broken, I began the journey of survival and the search for a new life. Flannery O'Connor, who also suffered from lupus, described lupus as a journey. She said that lupus is more instructive than a trip to Europe but it is a trip you have to take entirely on your own. Illness is certainly instructive if you open your heart and mind to the learning, but I disagree with O'Connor that you have to go through it entirely alone. I have found many teachers along the way to guide and instruct me in this journey.

The Ugly Dress (Lupus)

By Linda

My ugly dress is ugly only to me.
Others say, "But you look so good."
I look in the mirror and don't see myself.
A person with lupus stares back at me.
Even though I have to wear this ugly dress,
I will dress it up with hope.
Hope pulls attention from the ugliness
And I feel pretty again.

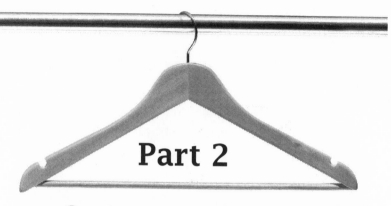

Part 2

Accessorizing the Ugly Dress

About Accessorizing

By Linda

N O MATTER WHAT you do or don't do, you will experience serious challenges in your life. No one is immune to life's problems. You may lose your health. You may lose your home, your loved ones, or even your freedom. Dr. Victor Frankl, a neurologist and psychiatrist, lost all of these.

In 1942, Dr. Frankl and his wife and parents were sent to Nazi concentration camps. Dr. Frankl was imprisoned for three years. During those years, he used his knowledge and skills to help himself and his fellow prisoners overcome the shock, grief, and despair of their losses. When Dr. Frankl was finally freed by the Americans in 1945, his sister was his only surviving relative. She had escaped the concentration camps and death by immigrating to Australia. Because of his suffering and that of others, Dr. Frankl reached the conclusion that everything can be taken from a man or a woman but one thing: the freedom to choose one's attitude in any given set of circumstances. In his 1946 book *Man's Search for Meaning,* he said, "Between stimulus and response there is a space. In that space is our power to choose our response. In our response lies our growth and our freedom."

Karen and I did not want our illnesses to define us or to dictate the quality of our lives. We wanted healthy, happy, and productive lives in spite of our illnesses. Instead of just accepting or reacting negatively to our ugly dresses of scleroderma and lupus, we decided to consciously and carefully choose accessories. Our accessories are the attitudes, beliefs, and behaviors we've embraced to help us manage our illnesses and live the lives we choose.

We decided at the onset to adopt a positive attitude toward our illnesses and other life challenges. As Karen said, "I don't want to be stuck with scleroderma *and* a bad attitude."

We also decided that we would not whine (or at least not to everyone and not all the time), and we would not ask, "Why me?"

My favorite athlete is Arthur Ashe. He was a world tennis champion in the 1970s and he died of AIDS at a very young age. When he was asked by a fan if he wondered why God had given him AIDS, he responded, "There are fifty million children around the world starting to play tennis. Five million learn to play tennis. About five hundred thousand learn professional tennis. Fifty thousand make it to the circuit and five thousand reach the Grand Slam. Fifty reach Wimbledon but only two make it to the finals. When I was holding the Wimbledon Cup, I didn't ask God: Why me? So why now, when I'm in pain, should I be asking, Why me?"

Although Karen and I accept that it's not realistic to keep a positive attitude, think "right" thoughts, and do the "right" things all the time, we try to stay balanced. We don't allow ourselves to stay too long in a negative state. We do this by choosing not to react immediately to what happens to us. Instead, we've learned to pause, assess, and then choose our reactions and our actions. We call this process "accessorizing."

Accessorizing is not about trying to deny, shut out, or control your emotions. It's about becoming more aware of and knowledgeable about what you're feeling and thinking so that you can have less emotional reactivity. Dwelling too long on negative thoughts and feelings without processing them and moving on can suck your energy and impact all your relationships—including the relationship with yourself. They negatively impact your health and well-being by affecting the immune and nervous systems. Bringing thoughts and feelings into awareness is not a passive process. By noticing what you're thinking and feeling, you gain insight that enables you to act in a more conscious and deliberate way. It allows you to choose the best response for the situation instead of being driven by fear, anger, or despair.

Pause

Pausing before reacting gives you the time and space to think, reflect, and gather strength. Ernest Bramah, an English author, said, "When a road ends abruptly, take small steps." Members of Alcoholics Anonymous use the acronym HALT as a reminder not to make decisions when they are *hurt, angry, lonely,* or *tired.* The pause, or time and space needed, will vary depending on the situation and your current mental and physical reserves. Whatever the time it takes, the pause is usually worthwhile. As Ovid, the prolific Roman poet, said, "Take rest. A field that is rested gives a beautiful crop."

Assess

Attitudes, thoughts, feelings, beliefs, moods, behaviors, and experiences are closely linked. Thoughts lead to feelings. Feelings affect your mood. The mood you're in may affect your behavior. All of these impact your health and well-being. So, it's important to ask yourself the following questions before making important decisions: What am I feeling? What am I thinking? What is my current mood? What attitudes, behaviors, or habits might have contributed to my current situation? Do I have the physical and mental stamina to move forward now or do I need a few minutes, days, weeks, or months before I am able to move forward? Do I need support or help from others in order to move forward? What is important in my life? What are my personal values and principles? What are my priorities? What options are available to me?

Choose

After pausing and assessing your current reality, it is equally important to *consciously* and *carefully* choose the response that is best for you. Your choices will be simpler if you have taken the time to define a personal set of values and principles to guide your decisions. Accessorizing is not a one-time event. It is a life-long process of personal growth. It involves becoming aware of your thoughts, feelings, moods, and behaviors; deciding how you want your life to be; and then making choices that support a balanced and fulfilling life.

In the following chapters, Karen and I discuss the strategies we use on a daily basis to manage our illnesses and our lives. Our strategies have evolved from our process of accessorizing and encompass our chosen attitudes, beliefs, and behaviors. As individuals, Karen and I are similar but different. Likewise, the choices we make and the strategies we use are similar but different. There is no "one-size-fits-all" solution. We've organized our strategies into the following categories: managing feelings, managing time and energy, navigating the healthcare system, managing perceptions, and achieving overall health and well-being.

Managing Feelings

Look for the Yellow Buoys

By Linda

WHEN WE'RE IN the midst of a crisis, whether it's the loss of our health or some other significant loss, we naturally feel overwhelmed. We assume we have to do everything at once instead of breaking things down into small, manageable steps. We often flounder about, unable to make *any* decision because *every* decision seems too big. I was certainly that way!

Until the diagnosis of lupus, I felt in charge of my life although I never took my health or good fortune for granted. I ate well, exercised, didn't smoke or drink, got plenty of sleep, and generally took good care of myself. Likewise, I was a conscientious and hardworking wife, mother, and employee. I guess I thought by doing all these things, I could control my little part of the world and prevent bad things from happening. But suddenly, instead of feeling in control I was totally out of control, despite all my best efforts. I was sick with lupus and the effects of high-dose steroids; my precious sister was gone; and my husband was divorcing me. At the same time I was losing the home I loved, my sanctuary, because it was too big and too expensive for me to manage alone. And my adored and only son was moving to Oregon, thousands of miles from me in South Carolina.

One night I wrote in my journal, "I feel as if I've been tossed into a raging sea and can't swim. I can see the shore and want very much to get there but I'm too weak and too tired to try." This was a powerful image for me because it highlighted my feelings of fear, aloneness, and powerlessness.

But I finally realized that these feelings were keeping me frozen. I knew there was help and support all around me, including family and friends, if I just looked and asked for it. It was then that I began to imagine my support system as bright yellow buoys scattered throughout the water. I realized that I didn't have to swim all the way to shore alone. All I had to do was reach for the nearest yellow buoy. Eventually, I'd reach the shore and be whole again.

I've come to think of yellow buoys as things to hold onto when life gets a little rough. They give me time to think, reflect, and gather strength, wisdom, and courage so that I can keep going. A yellow buoy is not always a person. It may also be a particular quote, belief, book, or poem—*whoever or whatever* keeps me afloat in my time of crisis. The yellow buoys that kept me afloat during that most difficult period included recognizing and exercising my power to choose, professional counseling, a support group, family and friends, and grace and spirituality.

Recognizing and Exercising the Power of Choice

My healing was initially stalled because I was stuck in victimization. I felt very sorry for myself and failed to recognize and exercise my own power to choose. After my husband announced his decision to get a divorce, he invited a real estate agent over to discuss selling our home. Pam (not her real name) was a neighbor in our subdivision and had been chosen entirely by Mike. I didn't know her well, but I still remember the humiliation of the day she came to list our home. Mike was completely in charge. He had arranged the appointment time and did all the talking on the pretense of helping me because I was "too sick." I cried the entire time she was there. I felt completely victimized and not at all a part of the process.

Months went by and the house had not sold. I didn't believe Pam was acting aggressively on my behalf, and I knew I needed to sell the house quickly in order to move forward with my new life. Little by little, I realized that I was giving away too much power to this real estate agent and to Mike, and it was keeping me in a victim position. Therefore, one of the things I did to move forward in my life was to take back my power of choice!

I looked for a new real estate agent, one I could trust and could work with as a partner. Henrietta, my new agent, blew into my life like a fresh wind. She owned her own realty company, and when she came to my house for the listing process, she made it clear that she usually sent a listing agent instead. However, she said that for some reason, she felt compelled to handle the listing of my house. Instead of assigning me to one of her agents after she took the listing, she decided to work directly with and for me. She guided me through the entire process of selling my house and buying a new home.

I've learned that self-healing begins with making your own decisions—about what to wear, what to do, and who you want to be. When you relinquish your power to choose, you keep yourself in a victimized position and healing won't take place.

Counseling, Psychotherapy, Talk Therapy

When going through any kind of life trauma, we need to feel a sense of mourning, loss, and fear, but the goal is to experience the feelings and move through them so we can emerge stronger. If we feel that we have to cover up every negative emotion, we usually can't get beyond those feelings.

A counselor or therapist is trained to help you understand your feelings and assist you in changing your thoughts and behaviors as necessary. Therapy can help decrease your depression, anxiety, and other symptoms such as pain and fatigue. Research increasingly supports the idea that emotional health and physical health are linked and that therapy can improve our overall well-being.

Selecting a therapist is a very personal matter because a therapist who works well with one person may not be a good choice for another. If you find that a therapist seems cold and uninterested or just doesn't seem to be helpful, talk to the therapist about this. If that doesn't work, consider another therapist.

According to the National Institutes of Mental Health, there are many kinds of psychotherapy or talk therapy, and there is no one-size-fits-all approach. The type of therapy that was helpful to me is called Cognitive Behavioral Therapy or CBT. It is a way to help you understand your current problems and how to solve them. The therapist helps you to identify distorted or unhelpful thinking patterns, recognize and change inaccurate beliefs, and then change your behaviors accordingly. Many studies have shown that CBT is a particularly effective treatment for depression, especially minor or moderate depression.

During the many months of my husband's and my separation and subsequent divorce, I chose to continue with the therapist Mike had initially chosen. He rejected her after only a couple of visits because she didn't confirm his perceptions of me. I chose to stay with her because of her competence, warmth, and caring. She gave me a safe place to vent all my feelings and helped me process the grief from my sister's death and the divorce, as well as the grief related to having a chronic illness.

Support Groups

The emotional pain of a divorce negatively affected my lupus. I felt as if my partner of nearly three decades had been surgically removed from my life, and the surgery left me raw and bleeding. A friend of mine had recently gone through a very difficult divorce and invited me to attend a divorce support group called "Rebuilding When Your Relationship Ends." I had very little energy at that point in my life and did not want to waste an ounce of it participating in "pity parties." Unfortunately, that was the perception I had of support groups.

I had never before participated in a support group and didn't know what to expect. My friend assured me that this particular support group focused on helping people take control of their lives and learn to make better choices; I was relieved to find that the group lived up to this promise and more. The Rebuilding Process, as specifically defined by this group, is based on a book by Dr. Bruce Fisher and Jere Bierhaus. The emotional stages one has to work through in a divorce are much the same as in any grief process, including grief over the loss of your health. The stages include denial, anger, bargaining, letting go, and acceptance. The Rebuilding Process presents a practical framework based on nineteen rebuilding blocks to help you understand and work through your emotions.

In addition to the learning that takes place in support groups, these groups can offer a warm and understanding atmosphere and another safe place to voice your pain and grief. A safe and supportive environment frees you to explore your feelings and fears with nonjudgmental and sympathetic others. Shakespeare said that you need to give words to sorrow because if you don't, the grief not spoken will cause your heart to break! If you are not physically able to attend a support group or you can't find one in your area, online support groups are also helpful.

I do have a caution to offer about support groups, however. Some people cling to their pain longer than necessary because they believe that if they give up their pain, they will have to give up the support and the sense of belonging. Carolyn Myss warns of this dynamic in her book *Why People Don't Heal and How They Can*. She says the dynamic of staying wounded calls to mind a saying by Buddha: "My teachings are a raft meant to help you cross over the river. Once you get to the other shore, set them down and go on with your life." We are not meant to stay wounded. We are meant to learn, to grow, and to move on.

Some may wonder why I didn't initially join a lupus support group. As I mentioned earlier, I had very little energy, and I was fortunate to have close friends with lupus and scleroderma (Robbie and Karen) who provided the sounding board and support I needed for the lupus issues. Later, when I was much stronger, I joined a local support group for lupus. I found it to be very helpful. The emphasis is on learning about the illness and better ways to manage it.

Family and Friends

Our culture places a lot of emphasis on becoming an independent person, and most of us fight hard to maintain that independence. Accepting support from others can be hard, but it can actually prove helpful not only to you but to those who are providing the support.

My mother and sisters live in different states (Alabama and Michigan). I live in South Carolina. They were very concerned about me, especially because my sister, Vickie, had died unexpectedly a few months before I was diagnosed with lupus. Vickie had died alone and many miles from family. Now I was also sick, alone, and many miles away. My family was frightened and they felt helpless.

My youngest sister, Janice, was especially distraught. She couldn't leave her daughter, Erin, who also was dealing with chronic health problems to come to South Carolina to be with me. In her inimitable way, she warned me that I absolutely, positively could not die. She said, "I've already lost one sister and I will not lose another one so soon! If you die, I swear I'll follow you all the way to hell and drag you back by the hair of your head." And I'm quite sure she would have! I've always joked with Janice's children that I might be the oldest sibling, but their mother is definitely the boss.

My mother, who is hard of hearing, has never quite understood that my disease is called "lupus." She refers to it as "Lucas." She always asks, "How's Lucas doing?" Sometimes I feel like saying, "Lucas is alive and well. Me, I'm not so great!"

My friends, my colleagues and staff, and even patients of the health center where I worked were also concerned about me when I was first diagnosed with lupus and was suffering from both the illness and high-dose steroid treatment. So many of these wonderful people showed caring in countless ways. It seemed that just when I needed support, it would appear in the form of a phone call, a funny or encouraging card, or beautiful flowers to brighten my day.

When I returned to work, my usually shy and unassuming office assistant said, "I've taken it upon myself to make some changes around here. I've rearranged some of the rooms so that you will have a quiet and private place to rest." I had to use that room many times over the next few years and will always be grateful for her wisdom and initiative on my behalf.

Even though I'm by nature a very independent person, my illness has taught me to ask for help when I need it and to graciously accept help when it is offered.

Grace and Spirituality

I believe in a Higher Power although I cannot describe Him or Her. I just have a certainty that there is a force greater than I and greater than the collective might of other humans.

When I was in the hospital in 1997 for lupus, I thought I might actually die. I prayed for grace even though I wasn't really certain at the time what grace looked or felt like. I just knew I needed lots of help to keep going. My friend Janet, who lost her husband to cancer when he was very young, says that grace is like being held aloft on soft pillows by a circle of friends. I now believe that grace fills you with the sense that no matter what happens you will receive the strength and the courage to deal with it.

While I was still in the hospital, I received a card from Terry, the driver of the university's mobile health unit. Terry is also a pastor of a local church and worked for the university part time. Terry wrote that he and his congregation were praying for my recovery. He also stated that he prayed I would receive a "peace that passes all understanding."

For the first time in my life, I actually felt completely peaceful despite the high levels of steroids coursing through my body. My fears about death, concerns about my husband's coldness, and concerns about the lupus began to seem manageable. I remember feeling that I would be okay with death. I didn't want to die and I didn't want my loved ones to be sad, but I knew I had lived my life the best I knew how. I believe that once you overcome your fear of death, life is much easier to live. I experienced a serenity that cushioned me during the months ahead while I struggled to get through the grief of divorce and learn to live a full life in spite of illness.

Many health professionals recognize that spirituality contributes to health and well-being. Definitions of spirituality vary but often refer to an individual's search for meaning in life. Some people get in touch with their spirituality through participation in organized religion. Others get in touch with their spirituality through connections to family, nature, or possibly the arts. I believe that a spirit or God force lives within each of us. It is always available and can be called upon whenever we need help. I believe that grace is a manifestation of that God force. Have you ever agonized over a situation for days or months and then you read a quote from a magazine or have a chance meeting with a stranger and suddenly you see the situation clearly for the first time? Or perhaps you have a dream that reveals to you issues that you didn't know were troubling you. These two situations are examples of serendipity, finding valuable or agreeable things that you had not searched for. I believe that grace often shows up in the form of serendipity. It is the "God within" that tries to connect the wisdom and guidance of our unconscious to our consciousness.

My experience has taught me that when you have a chronic illness, there are many times when you need comfort and help. During those times, you can sit alone and be despondent or you can choose to look for a yellow buoy. Yellow buoys give you something to hold onto while you think, reflect, and gather strength, wisdom, and courage so that you can keep going.

There is an old saying that resonates with me: "If you want milk, don't park your stool in the middle of a field and expect the cow to back up to it." Sometimes you have to take your pail and go find the cow. Seek out whoever or whatever keeps you afloat in your times of crisis. Remember that yellow buoys are not always people. You might find just the support you need in a book, a favorite poem, or other comforts in your life.

Managing Feelings
Call in the Helicopter

By Linda

*A*FTER MY HOSPITALIZATION in May, I tried to return to as normal a routine as possible in spite of illness and grief. I continued to work, although only a few days a week. However, I was barely able to function while at work because of the fatigue. I felt guilty about my inability to truly be a leader to my team. Although my staff, the dean, and my colleagues all assured me that I was doing a great job, I still felt I was letting them down. I told my friends that I felt as if I had a Corvette engine in a Ford Pinto body! My mind was full of ideas and plans but my body simply wouldn't cooperate.

My doctor gently suggested that I consider taking an indefinite leave of absence or quit my job and apply for disability so that the lupus could get better. In addition to the prednisone and placquenil, he prescribed Imuran, another immunosuppressant. I was resistant to all his suggestions, but especially to taking a leave of absence or applying for disability. Wouldn't that be giving up? Frank Stanton in his poem "Keep a-goin'" says, "If you strike a rose or thorn, keep a-goin'. If it rains or if it snows, keep a-goin'." I had always lived my life with that philosophy—no matter what happens, keep putting one foot in front of the other and keep moving forward.

On Sunday, October 19, I crashed. I had spent the day before with my friend and coauthor, Karen. We went house hunting in the morning and had a great time. She showed me the house she was considering buying. (She later bought that house and still lives there.) We enjoyed the beautiful fall day and went to a nice restaurant for a late lunch. While eating lunch, I started to feel ill and told Karen that I had to leave. By that night, I knew I had an upper-respiratory infection in addition to everything else. I didn't feel like getting out of bed to do anything, even to prepare soup or toast.

I wrestled with lots of feelings that night and the following day, but the most prevalent was fear. What if I let go and took a leave of absence? Would I lose my job? What if I took my sister Janice's offer to go to her home to recover? Would I ever want to leave the comfort of my sister and other extended family to return to living alone? Was I being a victim and seeking rescue?

I thought of the peacefulness of death. Wouldn't it be easier to just end my life? I had a lake behind my home. I visualized just walking calmly into it. I didn't believe I would actually commit suicide because of the pain it would cause my loved ones, but the thoughts scared me. When I look back on it, suicide by drowning was an absurd concept and shows the depth of my despair. I'm horrified of water and could not have walked peacefully into a lake. Someone would have had to sedate me, tie me up, and throw me in.

Sunday afternoon, I called my counselor, Marianne, in desperation and tears. I said, "I feel like a wounded soldier in the middle of a minefield. Parts of my body have been blown away and I am bleeding and weary. I am afraid to take another step for fear of hitting another mine. I don't want to give up, but I know if I don't get out of this minefield I'll bleed to death from my wounds." I also told her my sister Janice had suggested that I go to her home for a while, but I was afraid that would be giving up.

Marianne said, "Linda, when you're wounded and in the middle of a minefield, the thing to do is call in a helicopter. The helicopter will lift you out of danger and take you to a safe location until you can heal. Janice is your helicopter!" Marianne continued to assure me that it takes strength to admit when you've done all you can do. She said that I would also be giving a gift to my sister who was worried about me and yet couldn't leave her other responsibilities to care for me.

My favorite poet, Rumi, who lived in thirteenth-century Turkey, said that if you're helpless and dumbfounded and unable even to say yes or no, then a stretcher will come from grace to gather you up. At that moment I was totally helpless and dumbfounded, so I did as Marianne suggested and called in the helicopter.

I arranged a leave of absence with my doctor and the university. A few days later, friends drove me to meet Janice in Atlanta. I truly felt that Janice came from grace with a stretcher that day and gathered me up. She drove me to south Alabama where I lived with her and her family for five weeks.

They and the rest of my extended family refused to let me do anything more strenuous than make my bed. It was a wonderful period of rest and comfort. I played tea party every afternoon with my great nieces who taught me many things, especially patience and the joy of living in the present moment. I also learned more about setting boundaries, even with those I love. If you don't set boundaries with a four-year-old and a two-year-old, you'll be playing tea party for days on end. The girls always greeted me simply with, "Tea potty, Aunt Linda?"

One day, an adult niece was driving me to visit my mother. She was known for driving fast and maybe a little distractedly. However, with me in the car, she was the model driver. She kept asking, "Am I going too fast, Aunt Linda? Are you okay?" I realized that my usually boisterous niece was treating me like a precious and fragile Fabergé egg. In fact, my whole family had treated me this way during my stay. I had had the benefit of complete rest and relaxation for several weeks and the lupus had indeed improved, but it had not gone away as I had hoped. I knew then that I might have to live the rest of my life with the constraints of lupus.

I also knew I had reached the point that I could resume life on my own. I returned home a few weeks later.

It is often a huge challenge to accept that you need help and then actually admit it to someone else. But dealing with a chronic illness naturally leads to feelings of uncertainty, grief, sadness, anger, or fear, and these feelings can lead to depression. In fact, depression *often* accompanies chronic illness. You may not have a Janice in your life, but there are probably resources you have not considered. "Calling in a helicopter" takes courage because it means admitting your helplessness during a crisis. It is a step beyond reaching for a yellow buoy (bigger help for bigger problems), but sometimes you need more than a little support.

If you reach the point in your life when you are desperate, feel like giving up, and don't know who else to call, remember the National Suicide Hotline at 1.800.273 TALK (8255). Your call will be routed to one of over a hundred crises centers nationwide. This is a free and confidential service. The Hotline is available 24/7 to anyone who is suicidal or in emotional distress. Just talking to someone who is skilled in listening may help you to feel less alone and less anxious, allowing hope to return.

Managing Feelings

Tame the Angry Dobermans

By Linda

*F*RANKLIN DELANO ROOSEVELT said in his inaugural address that the only thing we have to fear is fear itself. If we are honest, most of us live our lives in fear: fear of abandonment, fear of failure, fear of death, and fear of the unknown or unidentified fear objects (UFO's). Fears that are unidentified are often vague and irrational. If we don't identify and deal with these fears, they can keep us in a constant state of hypervigilance, always expecting something bad to happen.

During the first few years of my illness, I'm not certain if I was more afraid of lupus or of the drugs prescribed to treat it. Earlier in my nursing career, I had seen the devastating effects of lupus on many patients. I was also keenly aware that drugs sometimes do as much harm as the illnesses they're used to treat.

One day during a visit to my rheumatologist, I felt very ill but was reluctant to tell the doctor how bad I felt because I didn't want him to pour on more medication. Unlike my usual persona of stoicism when visiting a doctor, I started crying and I told him how frustrated I was. I finally explained, "I'm afraid if I tell you how bad I feel, you'll say I'm going into a flare and will increase the prednisone or prescribe yet another toxic drug. I'm tired of drugs and more drugs. It's gotten to the point that I don't know whether I feel like hell because of the lupus or I feel like hell because of the medicines. On the other hand, if I don't tell you exactly how bad I feel, the lupus may get out of control and I'll have to go back to the hospital."

My doctor replied, "I understand. You are walking a high, narrow fence and there is an angry Doberman on either side."

Robert Louis Stevenson said that it is the first part of intelligence to recognize our precarious estate in life, and it is the first part of courage not to be at all abashed by that fact. Life *is* precarious. There *are* angry Dobermans out there. However, as human beings, we have the unique capacity to evaluate our fears and put them in perspective.

Fear can be a gift when it alerts you that something is wrong. In the animal world, fear is essential for survival because it triggers the flight-or-fight mechanism. However, even though a fear may be real, it doesn't always imply real danger. Not all fears require us to flee or to fight.

Fears can keep you from living a full and joyful life. Instead of just living with your fears, it is important to study and learn from them. Closely examine the fear and understand why you are feeling it. Learn to distinguish real dangers from perceived ones. When you feel afraid, ask yourself questions such as, "What's the worst thing that can happen?" "What are the odds that my fear will actually become reality?" "What can I do to tame the angry Dobermans?"

Knowledge is an antidote to fear, so learning all you can about your fears is one way to tame them. I learned everything I could about each of the medications prescribed and about my disease. I also found it helpful to talk to others who had been taking the same medications for a long time. By reading and talking to others, I could carefully weigh the risks and benefits of a new medication.

Writing your fears down on paper sometimes helps to put them in perspective. Reframing the fear is another strategy. Reframing is a process of looking at a situation through a different lens. I learned to reframe the way I viewed my medications. Instead of seeing them as poisonous and doing possible harm to my body, I began to view them as tools to help calm the lupus and to improve my quality of life.

In some instances, you just have to move forward in spite of your fear. If you face your fears, you can channel your energy into something more productive. Trust yourself and your inner strength. Know that whatever happens, you'll muster the resources to deal with it. I saw a sign once that said courage isn't always a roar—sometimes it's just a quiet voice in the middle of the night that says, "I'll try again tomorrow."

Managing Feelings

Catch the Wave

By Linda

W HEN I WAS in the first grade, our teacher, Miss Wiggins, took the class to the local movie theatre to see Walt Disney's animated feature *Alice in Wonderland.* My family did not own a television at that time and I had never seen a movie. I was expecting a wonderful adventure and lots of fun!

All was well until Alice went down the rabbit hole. As she went down the hole, she experienced all kinds of weirdness. She grew very large. Then she shrank to a size so small that she could go through a keyhole. I was frightened. What would happen next to poor Alice?

After a while, Alice started crying. I started crying. Alice cried louder. I cried louder. Miss Wiggins moved me to the seat next to her, hoping to comfort and quiet me. But as things got "curiouser and curiouser" for Alice, I started to wail! Miss Wiggins then moved me to her lap. I was still terrified and still wailed. Eventually, she had to call my mother to come get me. I probably ruined the outing for my classmates, and I most certainly ruined it for Miss Wiggins.

When I was first diagnosed with lupus, I felt like Alice when she went down the rabbit hole. I didn't know what to expect from one moment to the next. That's the way it is with lupus and other autoimmune diseases—very unpredictable. One day you're feeling okay, the next day you're very sick, maybe even unable to get out of bed.

I don't like unpredictability. It has always made me anxious. Maybe it goes back to my childhood when I often had to worry about my dad coming home drunk and creating chaos. It was so much nicer when I could go to sleep knowing that he would not be home that night so I could relax. But no matter how much I dislike unpredictability, it's a fact of life. Still, there are different ways of facing unpredictability and other obstacles in life. When I was going through the divorce, the counselor asked me to describe my personality and my ex-husband's personality. I said, "I am like a willow. I may look fragile but I'm not. I can be beaten to the ground by the storms of life but I just bend–I don't break. Eventually, I get back up. Mike is like the oak. He has a façade of strength but he doesn't bend, and that's his weakness."

The unpredictability with lupus and other autoimmune

illnesses is hard to get used to. I know a young woman who was diagnosed with lupus in her twenties. She became seriously ill, almost died, and was then incapacitated for many months. The lupus then went into a quiet period that lasted for about ten years. During that time, she had no symptoms and was on no medications. In her early thirties, without warning, she went into another severe lupus flare. The flare manifested as a stroke that was followed shortly by another stroke. While recovering from the strokes, her kidneys failed. She was in the hospital for weeks fighting for her life. Then she was in rehabilitation therapy for many months to overcome residual paralysis on one side of her body. I'm happy to say that she has now recovered most of her former functional ability.

Thankfully, my lupus has never been that severe. I have not had serious organ damage and I've only been hospitalized twice since diagnosis. However, even with mild or moderate autoimmune illnesses, the unpredictability is there. It's hard to plan anything, even if it's just a week away, because you don't know what you'll feel like at the time. You can become very isolated unless you have friends and family who understand and accept that you may have to cancel at the last minute.

The lack of predictability with lupus has at times had a negative effect on my job and my ability to create a dynamic vision and lead my team. There have been times when I've been reluctant to commit to a long-term project because I wasn't sure I would be able to fulfill my commitment. Once I was working with a colleague from another discipline on an important grant. With only a few days before the deadline and the grant still incomplete, I had a flare and couldn't continue. The grant was very important to our respective colleges, and it was also important professionally for my colleague and me. Fortunately, Dina and I had collaborated throughout the process, so she was able to complete the grant without my assistance and submit it.

One day when I was in the midst of a flare and feeling particularly frustrated about all the things I couldn't do, I thought about surfers I've observed over the years, such as my ex-husband. During the early years of our marriage, we lived in California. My ex-husband loved surfing so we went to the beach several times a week. I often sat and watched as he and dozens of other surfers paddled out to the deep and then sat on their surfboards patiently, sometimes for long periods, waiting to catch just the right wave. When that *right* wave appeared, they rode it joyfully as far as it would take them, the whole thing usually lasting only a few seconds. Then they paddled back to the deep and started the process all over again.

One of the ways I've learned to manage the unpredictability of lupus is by thinking of myself as a surfer who patiently awaits the next "good" wave. I think of the flares and quiet periods as similar to the ebb and flow of the waves in the ocean. Just as the surfer can't control the ebb and flow of the ocean, I can't control the lupus flares. I have to adapt. Charles Darwin said that it's not the strongest or smartest who survive in this world but those who are the most adaptable. Adaptability means flexibility, the ability to go with the flow instead of fighting it. It means awareness of and accep-tance of the present situation and the ability to make the best of it. When I'm in a quiet period, I relish doing the things I enjoy. When I'm in a flare, I use the time to rest, reflect, and gather strength in order to catch the next good wave.

Managing Time and Energy
Pay Attention to the Canaries

By Karen

EOPLE WITH AUTOIMMUNE diseases remind me of the canaries that coal miners used to take with them into the mines. The canaries were more sensitive to the odorless, colorless, poisonous gasses that could be present in the mines, and their smaller bodies would die quickly when they encountered the gasses. The canaries' deaths allowed the miners to know there was danger in the mine and gave them the chance to get out before they were hurt.

Today's fast-paced, frenzied, stress-drenched society is

like the poisonous gas in the mine, and those of us with auto-immune diseases seem to be the canaries. For some reason, our immune systems falter under the stresses of today's life-style. Perhaps we lack the proper buffers to endure them, or our capacity to tolerate such stresses is smaller. Regardless of whether it is the cause, catalyst, or both, stress seems to have an important relationship with autoimmune diseases. Every person I have talked with who has an autoimmune disease has a story to tell about a particularly stressful phase in life that occurred near the time of the disease's development.

We're all subjected to stress at some level, but I wonder if people with autoimmune diseases are perhaps giving the rest of the world a warning: "Something is toxic here, and as the toxicity increases or you get weaker, the environment is going to make you sick." It may just happen earlier in people with autoimmune disease. The better we understand auto-immune diseases, the better we can help all people avoid the negative effects of the stresses of modern life.

We all have early warning signs that our body sends us when stress rises to toxic levels. I know that I am moving into toxic levels of stress when my hands and feet swell. If I miss more than one day of physical activity or sit at the computer for several hours without taking a break and moving around, my feet become swollen blocks of flesh and my fingers become like sausages.

The most frightening sign my body sends me is the icy-hot burning sensation I feel in my forearms, lower legs, and face. My body couldn't send me a clearer message about what is toxic for me. This sign tells me that I have put my body in harm's way. Sometimes I feel this sign under acute stress situations such as when a car pulls out in front of me unexpectedly. But most often, I feel this after several weeks of pressure at work accompanied by inadequate rest, no exercise, and too much eating out. When I ignore the quiet message of swelling, my body starts yelling at me with fire. What scares me most about this sign is that whenever I feel it, I know I am hurting myself internally. My lungs, GI tract, and heart are being damaged because my immune system goes into overdrive after being in a toxic environment for an extended period of time. And without exception, my first thought—no matter how important the project I'm involved in seems—is always, "This is not worth dying for!"

It's important to learn what your early warning signs are and the circumstances that trigger them. The better you get at reading them, the better you can protect yourself. Of course you have to do more than detect them. Before your canary falls over dead, you have to get yourself out of the mine! Too often, we simply ignore the signs and stay in the toxic environment.

There seems to be a general disconnect today between our lifestyle habits and work values, on one hand, and what our bodies need in order to be healthy on the other. There are so many marvelous things that come with modern life: improved communication, transportation, convenience, and variety. We have so much available to us, yet as a society, we do so little to help people adapt by making wise choices or balancing it all healthfully.

I heard something on television recently that struck me as a humorous but pointed truth: "You can't pour five pounds of sugar into a one-pound bag." Isn't this exactly what we try to do with time and energy each day in today's society? We keep pouring and pouring as if the sugar will eventually figure out how to fit in the bag or the bag will miraculously become more than it is. We are so habituated to the rush and urgency of modern life that we often don't even question it. We keep pouring time and energy into the toxic mix—and it is killing us.

I recall a line from a 1970s Helen Reddy song: "I know too much to go back and pretend." When I was diagnosed with scleroderma, I knew that the stress I placed on myself during the previous years was not worth the price. I could no longer even pretend to buy into the belief that it is okay to program people to think that the only way they can be of worth in our society is if they push themselves to the brink of exhaustion so that they can have more stuff, bigger raises, and the "you work harder than anyone else here" award. It is thinking like this that got me into this ugly dress.

I look around year after year and continue to see so many of my friends and colleagues doing the same thing. I know how hard it is to face down the endless pressures that keep them working at pouring five pounds of time and energy into every one-pound day. I want to give them all T-shirts that read:

I gave my time, energy, and youth, and all I got was a lousy UGLY DRESS!

Managing Time and Energy

Know When to Hold 'Em and Know When to Fold 'Em

By Linda

T HE GUEST SPEAKER at a meeting of my lupus support group asked the audience, "What is your worst symptom with the lupus?" In a united and very loud voice, the audience responded resoundingly, "FATIGUE!"

I was a high energy person before lupus. Of course, I got tired at times, the kind of tired you feel when you've cleaned the house or worked in the yard, the kind that can be relieved with a short nap or a nice glass of iced tea. I had no concept of the debilitating fatigue that accompanies lupus and other chronic illnesses.

The fatigue I have with lupus does not go away with rest. It is so severe at times that it is sheer work just to hold my eyes open. Every movement takes concentration and effort. My ex-husband often teased me by saying that he was going to have "Too Tired Tig" carved on my tombstone. (Tig was his nickname for me, short for Tiggr.) The way I felt at the time, I didn't think he'd have long to wait.

The only thing I can compare to lupus fatigue is an episode of flu I had when I was in nursing school. I was so tired then that I did not care if I lived or died. I didn't have the energy to drink from the cup of cola that my mother kept putting to my lips and urging me to drink. The best I could manage was to sip occasionally and weakly through a straw. Mother even had to support me when I went to the bathroom.

If people without autoimmune diseases have ever had a severe case of the flu, they *might* have an idea of what it is like to have the kind of fatigue that is a common symptom of such illnesses. In my case, even on the days when I feel my best, the fatigue is there like background noise. I liken it to the constant hum of a sound machine that some people use to help them sleep. You become so accustomed to the hum that you don't really notice it until it stops or for some reason the rhythm changes, such as the overpowering fatigue that strikes during a flare.

Months after my lupus diagnosis, I was still trying to do things the same as before even though the fatigue was crippling. One day when returning to my office from an off-campus meeting, I drove around trying to find a place to park. Most college campuses are designed for pedestrians, as ours was, with traffic and parking limited except on the periphery. That day I drove around in circles for about fifteen minutes to no avail, getting more and more frustrated. Although my doctor had previously given me an authorization for a handicap placard, I had stubbornly refused to get one. What would people think? I didn't look sick enough to be handicapped!

For some reason, while driving around that day I finally realized that I was wasting energy that could be used for a better purpose. I imagined a deck of cards and realized that if most people are dealt ten energy cards a day, then a person with an autoimmune disease probably gets five to seven energy cards at best.

Simply getting up, eating, dressing, and driving to work were already using up several of my cards each day. I knew I had the choice of using more of my precious energy cards driving around trying to find a parking space at work day after day, or I could swallow my silly pride and get a handicap placard. I went that very day to the highway department and got a placard. I only had to use it for a few months at that time, but it made a difference in conserving energy when I needed it the most.

I have learned that with lupus I can't do everything I once did, and I certainly can't do the same things in the same way. I believe it's important to have strategies for managing energy wisely. The following strategies have been particularly helpful to me:

- Decide which things are most important and act on those priorities.

- Practice the fine art of discrimination and selectivity.
- Figure out how energy is being drained from your body and then plug those drains.
- Find ways to nourish both body and soul so that energy stores are replenished.

Decide Which Things Are Most Important and Act on Those Priorities

If you want to determine what is most important in your life, visualize your funeral. Stand in a corner and watch who comes and who is crying, and listen to what is being said. Decide if you want your eulogy to be about career accomplishments and acquisitions of wealth and status or about what you've meant in the lives of your family and friends.

I went through the funeral exercise a few years before the diagnosis of lupus. I even wrote a personal creed to serve as my compass and guide me when I lost direction because it is so easy to be pulled away from your priorities by the demands of everyday life. So I thought I had a pretty clear idea of what was important to me. In my creed, I stated that relationships with my loved ones would take priority above other things.

After I was diagnosed with lupus, I had to re-order my priorities. Even though my doctor had suggested several times that I consider applying for disability in order to better manage the lupus, I had no other source of income and very little savings, and my work contributed greatly to my sense of self-worth and well-being. I realized that work had to be very high on my list of priorities. Then I remembered an old Chinese proverb that basically says no matter how much wealth you have, if you lose your health, you have nothing. It became clear to me that health had to be my number one priority. Otherwise, I would not only be unable to work, but I wouldn't be able to truly enjoy or contribute to my valued relationships.

If you have trouble determining your priorities and the funeral exercise doesn't help, you might want to try the exercise called "Putting the big rocks in first." I've seen this demonstrated many times at management seminars. The seminar leader displays two large-mouth jars of equal size. He then displays two bags filled with an equal number of large and small rocks. In the first jar, he puts the small rocks in first. He then tries to put in the larger rocks, but no matter what he does, they simply won't fit. In the second jar, he carefully places the big rocks in first. Then he puts in all the small rocks. Amazingly, everything fits. He even pours in a bag of sand that fills the in-between spaces.

The big rocks are a metaphor for what's most important in your life. If you don't attend first to the things that are most important, you may not have the time or energy to deal with them. Your life will be filled with minutiae—the little rocks and sand in your jar.

Practice the Fine Art of Discrimination and Selectivity

The definition I found in the dictionary for discrimination is, "to make sensible decisions; to judge wisely." The dictionary provides an example of a person who collects rare books. The person can't collect all the rare books in the world. He or she has to be selective, to discriminate.

Like most of us, Anne Morrow Lindbergh, wife of Charles Lindbergh, was an extremely busy person with multiple demands on her time. She was a wife, mother of five children, and author of numerous books. In her book *A Gift from the Sea,* she described her life in America in 1925 as one with ever-increasing demands—not only family demands, but community demands and national and even international demands. She said that the interrelatedness of the world connects us constantly with more people than our hearts can hold and presents more problems and demands than the human body can stand. If this interrelatedness of the world was a matter of both interest and concern in 1925, think how much more so it is today.

When Mrs. Lindbergh needed time alone to reflect and regroup, she often went to a small island beach house. On one of her retreats, she walked on the beach the first day and avidly collected every beautiful shell she saw. Soon her pockets were filled and her hands were overflowing. She repeated the shell collecting on subsequent days. As her time at the beach came to a close, she sorted through and kept only a few of the shells. She realized that you cannot collect all the beautiful shells on the beach. You can collect only a few, and they are more beautiful if they are few. The same thing is true for other things as well.

The world is full of people to love and things to do. The world also constantly inundates us with the latest trends and changing values. How do we choose? We can decide to be governed by the world's values or learn to make decisions based on our own values and needs.

Before lupus, I was governed in part by the world's values and the world's measures of success. I was in a fast-paced work environment and was constantly seeking new challenges and bigger rewards. But I slowly realized that I wasn't living the way I wanted to live.

I took a long time to reflect before I wrote my personal creed. I thought about the things that are really important to me and the things that bring me the greatest peace and joy. I looked back over my life and considered the kinds of work that bring me the greatest satisfaction. It took me about three months before I could clearly define my personal values and priorities, but the personal creed I wrote has served me well for the last sixteen years. It has helped me to be more discriminating in my choices of friends, activities, and work. I now feel that I am governed by my own needs and values instead of those of others and the world at large.

Thomas Merton said, "To allow oneself to be carried away by a multitude of conflicting concerns, to surrender to too many demands, to commit one's self to too many projects, to want to help everyone in everything is to succumb to the violence of the times."

Figure Out How Energy Is Being Drained from Your Body and Plug Those Drains

Once you've decided the things that are most important in your life and learned the fine art of discrimination in your choices, then it's important to recognize and plug all the energy drains. Several common energy drains affect many of us:

- Dealing with certain people or things

- Holding onto negative emotions such as anger and resentment
- Living by artificially high standards and expectations
- Worrying about the future instead of living for the present
- Wearing a mask or playing a role

Dealing with certain people and things: Some people can drain you of energy. I have acquaintances who love to talk on the telephone for long periods of time. Sometimes, I don't have the energy to even hold the phone. I tried lying down when they called and just putting the phone to my ear, but it was still draining. Finally, I learned to courteously end the conversation in a reasonable time period.

Have you ever noticed how certain activities leave you feeling totally drained? Driving back and forth to the university five days a week was a huge energy drain for me. The commute took almost an hour each way. To figure out how I could continue working, I went to my dean and explained my situation. He was very caring and assured me that he would do whatever was necessary to help me continue in my role at the university. So I arranged with him and my staff to work from home one to two days a week. And to further conserve my energy, I sometimes stayed overnight in Clemson with friends instead of driving home at the end of the day.

If you are still employed, you may find that frequent interruptions will drain you of energy and keep you from achieving results. I was only in my office a few days a week, so I had to learn to be very productive in a shorter time frame.

I used the Franklin Covey Time Management Matrix to help me better organize and use my time. The matrix divides all activities into four quadrants:

- Important/Urgent (such things as crises or pressing problems)
- Important/ Not Urgent (preparation, crises prevention, values clarification, planning, relationship building)
- Not Important/Urgent (some phone calls, some meetings, some mail or reports, etc.)
- Not Important/Not Urgent (trivia, busywork, some mail or phone calls, procrastination)

Obviously, you will have to spend time managing the Important/Urgent situations but it's very easy to get caught up in trivia and busywork. If you learn to spend about 80 percent of your time on Important/Not Urgent activities such as clarifying your values, building your important relationships, and managing your overall health, you will have fewer crises and get a lot more accomplished.

Holding onto negative emotions: A huge energy drain for me was holding onto the pain of my losses. In his book *Emotional Resilience,* Dr. David Viscott describes three kinds of losses: 1) loss of a love, 2) loss of control, and 3) loss of esteem (such as loss of beauty, youth, and sexual allure). When you lose your physical and mental strength, you experience both loss of esteem and loss of control.

I had experienced all three kinds of losses. I had lost my marriage. I felt out of control because of all the changes taking place. The future I had counted on would not happen. Where would I live? Would I be able to continue working? Would the lupus get worse? My body, which I had cared for conscientiously over the years, had also betrayed me. I felt the loss of self-esteem not only because of the changes in my appearance, but also because of the loss of my physical and mental vigor.

I was hurt and angry that these things had happened to me. Anger is often a signal that you are being hurt, that your needs are not being met, or that your boundaries have been ignored. It's a legitimate emotion, and it's appropriate to feel anger when you've experienced a loss such as the loss of a love relationship or the loss of your health. However, feelings such as anger and resentment need to be vented and released because holding onto them keeps you from moving on. Until you do this, you can't reach acceptance, which is the final phase of dealing with loss.

Some people choose to hold onto anger and resentment just to show the world how badly they've been treated. This keeps them in a victim position. Others hold onto their pain because they're afraid of showing their vulnerability or they're afraid of losing control. *Me, hurt? Not me! I'm strong and invincible.*

Women, especially, have a hard time expressing anger. They've grown up with so many taboos against feeling and expressing anger that they sometimes don't even know when they're angry. Because of my childhood and my father's frequent and violent outbursts of anger, I was especially afraid of anger and its repercussions. I had to learn to trust that I could express and manage my anger in constructive instead of destructive ways.

Everyday anger, the type that comes up as part of the normal ups and downs of daily life, should be expressed when it occurs instead of letting it build. Learn to talk about your anger directly, firmly, and honestly. One constructive way to express anger is to use "I" messages instead of "you" messages. An example is to say "I'm angry" instead of "You make me angry." The first message identifies what *you're* feeling and keeps the responsibility for your feelings on you instead of another person. It is less likely to make the other person defensive.

When expressing anger, it's important to avoid sarcasm, which is derived from a word meaning "to tear flesh." Avoid name-calling or put-downs. Stick to the issue of the moment and don't dredge up things that happened in the past. My ex-husband often brought up in minute detail things that had happened years in the past. How could I possibly respond when I couldn't even remember what had happened the day before—certainly not details of an event that had happened weeks, months, or years past? The counselor told him that he was guilty of one of the biggest mistakes in a relationship—list-making.

Stored-up anger, which can occur with a divorce, the loss of your health, or other large events in your life, can be dealt with in many constructive ways. Any form of physical exercise can help you release anger, especially if you combine the exercise with other techniques. For example, when a friend was going through a divorce, her counselor told her to hit golf balls and imagine the golf balls as her husband's head or bounce a basketball and imagine the same thing. Physical exercise was closed to me, as it probably is to many of you, because of the extreme fatigue of lupus. I could hardly find the energy to get dressed, so running around the block or hitting a golf ball were not options.

I had to find other ways to release my anger, so I cried! Sir William Osler, a physician, said that if hurt doesn't find an outlet in tears, it may cause other organs to weep. If you can't cry, use your vocal cords. I wanted to scream out my hurt and anger but knew that if I screamed, my caring neighbors would think I was being attacked and call the police. One night I turned on the water faucet in the kitchen sink, turned on the garbage disposal, and screamed away my rage and frustration into the disposal. It helped and the police did not show up.

Writing down your feelings in letters or a journal or talking them out with people who care will also help you release them. I wrote many letters to my husband that I never mailed. In fact, I never intended to mail them. I just needed to vent, and pouring out my feelings in letters provided that catharsis.

I also used a technique called the "empty chair" where I pretended my husband was actually sitting across from me in an empty chair. I sat in front of him one night and told him how much I had been hurt by his actions and how disappointed I was that he had abandoned me at my weakest and worst. Actually, I called him every kind of derogatory name I could think of, believing that it's okay to use name-calling when no one else hears it! The balloon exercise is another way to release anger and other painful feelings. Write all your feelings on paper, then tie the paper to a balloon and let it go.

Forgiveness is the third phase of dealing with anger. It's

important when going through this phase that you forgive yourself as well as the person you think caused you harm. I realized that in addition to the anger I felt toward my husband, I was also angry at myself. How could I have been so stupid? Did my husband ever love me? Did I bottle up my hurt and anger over the years just to hold the marriage together? Had I caused the lupus? I blamed myself for my complicity in the loss of my marriage and in the loss of my health.

Forgiveness does not mean that what happened to you doesn't matter, and it doesn't mean that it is all right for someone to harm you. It simply means releasing the negative feelings you have about that event and the person or persons involved. Forgiveness lightens your load and frees up your energy for more productive efforts because when you truly forgive, you no longer carry the baggage of that negative experience.

If you find that you are constantly complaining about what happened to you, it may mean that you're still holding someone else responsible. You may be absolutely certain that the perceptions you hold about the behavior of the other person are totally right. You may feel completely jus-tified in your anger and the correctness of your judgment. However, when you're unforgiving, you *always* see yourself as innocent and others as guilty. Forgiveness is a means of changing your perceptions and letting go of whatever you think other people have done to you.

As anyone who has tried it knows, forgiveness is not a one-time decision. It's a process and it is not simple. It only comes as a result of confronting your pain. So feel your pain, anger, and resentment, but then work through your feelings in positive ways until you can forgive yourself and others. Then you'll be ready to move on.

I was incredibly hurt and angry when my husband asked for a divorce. Over time I have learned to accept it as something he had to do for himself. Since then, I have learned that many spouses choose to leave when a partner is diagnosed with a serious illness. Some estimates of well spouses who leave are as high as 75 percent. The well spouse may be experiencing many of the same emotions as the sick spouse: grief, anger, denial, and depression. The emotional needs of the well spouse are not always recognized by family or friends because the attention and concern is directed to the sick spouse. It is important for well spouses to reach out and support is available through organizations such as the National Family Caregivers Association (http://www.familycaregiver.org/) and the Well Spouse Association (http://www.wellspouse.org/).

One of my favorite birthday cards is by Mary Engelbreit and has a caption that reads, "Don't Look Back." The illustration is of a cheerful little girl walking jauntily along. She passes a fork in the road and chooses the fork with a directional sign that reads, "Your Life." The sign for the fork not taken says, "No longer an option." I kept this card on my refrigerator for many years because it signaled to me that I couldn't go back. I know that despite whatever role I played in the breakup of my marriage or the loss of my health, I can only learn from the experience and move forward.

Living by artificially high standards and expectations: I love a clean house! In the past, a clean house always meant vacuuming, dusting, mopping, and doing all the other chores in my cleaning routine at least once a week whether the house needed it or not. With the lupus, I had to compromise. There were times when I could clean nothing at all and times when I celebrated if I cleaned one room. I'm still not able to clean the house from one end to the other as I once did. Since I can't afford a housekeeper, I'm always on the lookout for tools to make cleaning easier. One tool I've found is the iRobot Roomba. This little robot vacuum cleaner has become one of my favorite things. You simply put him in a room, close the doors and let him work. (I find it interesting that I refer to Roomba as a "he." I guess it's because I've always wanted a man who would do housework.)

Another way I lowered my standards was to accept that a complete bath or shower every single day is not always necessary. I'm not saying you should neglect hygiene or personal appearance because it's important to your self-esteem—not to mention your relationships with other people—to be clean and well groomed. But there may be room to compromise on some of your routines. My sister Janice tells about spending summers with our grandmother, Mama Lowe. Janice said that sometimes after playing all day she was simply too tired to take a full bath before bed. Mama Lowe told her, "Just bathe the three F's: face, feet, and fanny ... in that order!" Think about all your routines. Are there ways to compromise and save energy that would still allow you to feel good about yourself?

I also lowered my standards and expectations about what others should or should not do by finally resigning my self-appointed position as manager of the universe. As the oldest of seven children, I always felt a sense of responsibility, not only for my siblings but for my mother and others as well. I felt it incumbent on me to try to solve everyone's problems or to fix things.

I especially tried to advise Mother regarding my brother because I felt he was using her. He often acted in irresponsible ways and Mother would then bail him out of the consequences. I got very angry and lost a lot of energy because she would never listen to my advice. Only after my own son was born did I finally realize that trying to interfere in any way with Mother's relationship with her son was complete arrogance. I acknowledged to Mother then that I realized her relationship with her son was hers alone and none of my business. My relationship with my brother was a separate issue, and I needed to work on it directly.

I realize now that my advice-giving and other interfering ways were the result of a need to control, to prevent bad things from happening. Illness and life in general have taught me that control is an illusion. Lao-tzu in the Tao Te Ching said, "Do you think you can take over the universe and improve it? I do not believe it can be done. Everything under heaven is a sacred vessel and cannot be controlled. Trying to control leads to ruin. Trying to grasp, we lose."

Worrying about the future instead of living in the present: When I was a teenager, we lived next door to my grandmother. Every afternoon in good weather, you could find Mama Lowe on her front porch in her rocking chair with her "spit" can nearby. (Her one indulgence and the only fault I knew about was dipping snuff.) She sat with her arms folded comfortably over her ample lap and rocked the hours away. Nothing seemed to bother her, so she was the perfect sounding board for my siblings and me. I would sit on her front porch and talk about things that were troubling me. Mama Lowe often said, "Linda, worry is like this rocking chair. It gives you something to do but gets you nowhere."

Over the years I've reflected on my grandmother's wisdom. It really makes no sense to endlessly worry. A Chinese philosopher said that birds of worry and care will fly above your head and you can't change that. However, you *can* prevent them from building nests in your hair.

Instead of dwelling on all the "What ifs," I've learned to think about my worries and sort them into two categories: things I can do something about, and things I can't. The Serenity Prayer has helped me many times to distinguish between the two: *God grant me the serenity to accept the things I cannot change, courage to change the things I can, and wisdom to know the difference.*

Another technique I've learned is to ask myself if there is any action I can take now or later to minimize the imagined consequences. If there is, then I make a plan and do it! But if there is nothing I can do to actually change things, then I ask myself if what I'm worried about is truly important. Will this matter in one hundred years? About 90 percent of all worries are unimportant, unlikely, or can't be resolved anyway.

So if you are worried about something, ask yourself how much of your limited energy the issue is really worth. Ralph Waldo Emerson said, "Some of your hurts you have cured and the sharpest you've even survived. But what torments of grief you've endured from evils which never arrived."

Wearing a mask or playing a role: We often use masks and act a role to protect ourselves from emotional pain or as a way to hide what we're really feeling. Most of us develop our masks because we think we won't be loved or accepted the way we *really* are. Wearing a mask or acting a role takes a great deal of emotional energy. I believe one of the most exhausting things in life is trying to be someone you're not.

Like most people, I didn't know I wore masks. I thought I was a very open and honest person, but as I explored myself and my contributions to the divorce and to my illness, I learned that I had worn a lot of masks.

One of the ways I coped as a child was to play "house." I can still visualize all the imaginary houses I set up in the various places we lived. I always played the wife, and my imaginary husband was basically the TV model of husband and father. No anger or fighting in my imaginary home! In that world, there was always enough money and we faced no major issues. I played in this imaginary world for hours at a time. It never mattered whether others played with me or not.

I see now that playing house was a coping mechanism for me. I could shut out what was real and retreat at will. I know in my marriage I wanted so much for it to work that I shut out a lot of my feelings and misgivings in order to keep the relationship intact. In retrospect, I created another playhouse.

Most of my life I had also acted the roles of good girl, good student, good wife, good patient, and even good divorcée because I was always trying to be what others needed me to be. Basically, I had been a people pleaser, always trying to do the right thing and get along. I realized that I had been carrying a tremendous burden by acting the way I thought I *should* instead of just being myself.

If you've ever worn a mask and then taken it off, you probably know the great feeling of freedom that comes with finally being yourself. It feels like unloading a tremendous burden, leaving you with a lot more energy to do other things. I might never have discovered the masks I wore but for the pain of the loss of my sister, husband, home, and health. As Kahlil Gibran said in *The Prophet*, "Your pain is the breaking of the shell that encloses your understanding... Much of your pain is self-chosen. It is the bitter potion by which the physician within you heals your sick self."

Find Ways to Nourish Your Body and Soul so that Your Energy Stores Are Replenished

When you're dealing with a chronic illness, getting the right amount of sleep and rest is critical. I think of sleep and rest as tools to manage my illness. I have found that I need a minimum of nine hours of sleep each night. I also have to rest at least thirty minutes in the afternoon. My doctor told me very early in my treatment that if I didn't get enough rest, I would have a flare. I tested that theory several times and found that he was right. If I push my body too hard and don't provide adequate recovery time, I pay for it with a flare.

Studies done at the National Institute of Neurological Disorders and Stroke have shown that the neurons that control sleep are closely linked to the immune system. The link between the nervous and immune systems is an important one. Cytokines, a type of protein found in the nervous system, are also part of the body's immune system and can trigger pain by promoting inflammation, even in the absence of injury or damage.

Some studies suggest that lack of sleep affects the immune system in detrimental ways. Sleep is necessary for our nervous systems to work properly. Too little sleep leaves us drowsy and unable to concentrate the next day. It also leads to impaired memory and physical performance and reduced ability to carry out complex activities such as math calculations.

If sleep deprivation continues, hallucinations and mood swings may develop. Some experts believe sleep gives neurons that are used while we are awake a chance to shut down and repair themselves. Without sleep, neurons may become so depleted in energy or so polluted with byproducts of normal cellular activities that they begin to malfunction. Sleep also may give the brain a chance to exercise important neuronal connections that might otherwise deteriorate from lack of activity.

So getting the right amount of rest and sleep is essential, but it doesn't really rejuvenate or energize me. It just enables me to keep going. To rejuvenate, I make choices that nourish both body and soul. Everyone is different, so what works for me may not work for you.

Personally, I find that being outside in nature, even if it's just a drive in the country or a quiet stroll, provides me with peace and renewal. Nature manages to sooth me whenever I'm afraid, lonely, or unhappy. When I'm outside in a place where I can be quiet and alone with the heavens, nature, and God, I am able to feel that all is as it should be and that God wants to see me happy.

Communion with animals is also restorative to me. When I was very ill with the lupus, I often just sat outside and observed God's majesty in all the living things around me. I live in a condominium community that doesn't allow unleashed pets, so I was very surprised the first time a yellow cat appeared in my yard. Each time I sat outside, the cat came around. I named him "CC" for Community Cat and began to look forward to seeing him.

"CC" was a feral cat and was very skittish around people, but if I stayed very quiet and still, he would come onto the steps beside me and occasionally brush against me. After awhile, he stayed with me even if I talked to him. I had never had an indoor pet and honestly had never liked cats, but I began to love this one. I made up my mind that I would adopt him, but then he stopped coming. Maybe he thought I didn't need him as much as I had earlier, or maybe someone else needed him more. All I know is that "CC" brought me great comfort.

Animals sometimes sense our needs even more than humans. The following poem by Saint John of the Cross and published in Dr. Wayne W. Dyer's book *Change Your Thoughts – Change Your Life* describes the wonder of communion with animals.

A Rabbit Noticed My Condition

I was sad one day and went for a walk;
I sat in a field.
A rabbit noticed my condition and came near.
It often does not take more than that to help at times —
To just be close to creatures who
Are so full of knowing,
So full of love
That they don't —
Chat,
They just gaze with their marvelous understanding.

Meditation is another means I've found to nourish my body and soul. My mind is like a "Chatty Cathy." It never shuts up, especially when I'm on lots of prednisone. Until lupus, I never took naps during the day. I hadn't needed to. My friend Robbie, who also has lupus, often chastised me for not resting enough. I said, "But Robbie, I sit down with a cup of tea and read a book. That's how I've always rested." She told me that wasn't enough and that I needed to "quiet the mind" to get the real benefit of rest.

It was extremely difficult for me to learn to quiet my mind. As John Milton said, "The mind is its own place, and in itself, can make a heaven of hell or a hell of heaven." Meditation can be a way of sealing yourself off from the stresses and annoyances of the outside world, a way to become disengaged from all the outside fears and distractions so that you can truly relax.

I have found many benefits to meditation. I am more peaceful and at ease, and my creativity flows. Things that didn't seem possible before often open to me after meditation. I feel more joyful and optimistic.

There are many books and tapes that will help you learn to meditate. For me, the easiest way to meditate is to focus on my breathing. You can do this while lying down or sitting in a relaxed position. Close your eyes and place your hands on your belly. Think of your belly as a balloon. As you breathe in, imagine the balloon filling up. As you breathe out, imagine the balloon deflating.

Meditation does not have to be difficult although it does take practice. I use the term "practice" loosely because many feel that by working to improve your meditation, you defeat the purpose. Think about a glass of muddy water. If you leave the glass alone, over time the water becomes clear. So just sit or lie in a quiet place and the mind will settle itself. When you first try meditation, you may become anxious or frustrated when your mind wanders. If you find your mind wandering from your breathing, don't be hard on yourself. Simply call your mind back to your breathing. Say something like, "Okay, I let my mind wander but now I'll try again."

Once you've learned to really focus on your breathing, you may find that repeating a mantra, prayer, or some kind of chant will help you improve your meditation practice. You can use any repetition of words that is meaningful to you. I use, "Peace. Be still." As I breathe in, I say the word, "Peace." As I breathe out, I say, "Be still."

It doesn't really matter what words or techniques you use. It's only important that you keep trying. You can also visualize a person or scene while you're repeating a chant.

Again, the specific visualization is not important as long as it is one that is peaceful and relaxing to you. I visualize one of my sisters with her arms outstretched and a big welcoming smile on her face.

Walking meditation is another way to focus your mind in the present and relieve some of your anxieties. It can be as simple as it sounds. Mark off a straight path of about twenty steps and then walk slowly back and forth along the path. Don't watch your feet. Just pay attention to the walking process by thinking about the actual movements as you walk: lift the leg, move the leg, place the foot.

A more formal approach to walking meditation is to use a labyrinth. The labyrinth is laid out as a single circular path to and from a center. Unlike a maze, it has no dead-ends or false passageways. When walking a labyrinth, you walk slowly and thoughtfully, one step at a time, from the beginning to the center. Some labyrinths have a resting place at the center for you to meditate and pray. Then you walk slowly back to the beginning.

Those of us with chronic illnesses are dealt a limited number of energy cards each day, so we need to know when to hold 'em and know when to fold 'em. As Robert Lewis Stevenson said, "Life is not a matter of holding good cards, but of playing a poor hand well."

The Wolf *

By Linda

A wolf lives inside me.
He stirs and I pay attention.
I once was a people pleaser.
Now, I'm a wolf pleaser too.

* Lupus is derived from a Latin word meaning wolf.

The Unwelcome Guest

By Linda

An angry wolf resides within.
His name is Lupus.
He's not my friend.
Be quiet, I say.
Please stay at rest.
When you're awake,
I can't be my best.
I will not give in
But I will compromise,
If you'll just curl back up
And close your eyes.

Navigating the Healthcare System

Become Your Own Advocate

By Karen

*T*WO OF THE most important things I have to continuously develop since the diagnosis of scleroderma are
knowledge and skills in managing my health. Your
knowledge and skills are applied in healthcare settings,
work settings, and social settings, and they will ultimately
determine how well you can advocate for yourself. A
research paper published in 2007 in a journal called *Disability and Rehabilitation* examined key components of living
with scleroderma and provided a summary of the informa-

tion newly diagnosed patients need for successful disease self-management (Mendeson and Poole, 2007). The authors titled their paper "Become your own advocate" and shared three themes that emerged as important for maintaining the highest quality of life possible:

- Learn everything you can
- Secure effective medical management
- Live your life

It is important to be able to communicate effectively with your health care providers. Become familiar with the language of your disease and keep a journal of your symptoms, drugs, physician visits, and questions for your physicians. Keeping a journal gives you a record of onset and length of symptoms and patterns that might occur seasonally that can help with preventing or better managing recurring problems. I find it very helpful to keep a journal, and it makes physician visits less stressful if I don't have to try to remember small details between visits. After more than nineteen years of having scleroderma, dates start running together, and I find it hard to remember who prescribed what and when.

Self-advocacy plays an important role not only in securing proper healthcare but also in exercising control in your disease management and avoiding a helpless mindset. Position yourself as co-manager with your healthcare provider and cultivate a relationship of mutual respect.

It is not easy to explain our relationship with our "healers." This relationship can take on so many forms: Child-Parent; Consumer-Provider; Mortal-God. It is endless. I remember hearing a story about a woman who had a chronically ill child. She was trying to explain to the child's doctor that something had changed about the child and she was worried. The doctor did not feel there was a need for concern and told the mother to not worry. In her fear and frustration, however, she challenged the doctor. She said, "No offense, doctor, but you're wrong. I know when something isn't right with this child. You see, she is my only patient. I am with her twenty-four hours a day, seven days a week. I know how she breathes. I know how she sleeps. I see everything—every day! I know when things are normal and I know when things are not normal. So, no offense, doctor, but you really don't know the patient like I do." That story sums up the way I feel about my relationship with my body and my disease … I am my *only* patient!

It takes a while to trust your "knowing" about your disease. It can be difficult at first to disagree with a medical authority's conclusion that nothing is wrong—or even that something is wrong—when you feel that the opposite is true. You don't want to offend someone you are so dependent on, and you might not know how to communicate what you are experiencing. You don't have the same tools the doctors have to defend your conclusion. But you must develop your knowledge and skills to become the primary caretaker for your well-being. This is not an easy job to have. You must read, think, and investigate. You must advocate. You must pay attention and remember details. You are the only one who can do this much and know this much about what is going on inside of you. It can be exhausting, but what alternative do you have?

I have come to understand that it is unrealistic, unfair,

and probably even naïve to think that a physician who sees hundreds and hundreds of people a year will remember all of the details of your situation or will track down small details and associated research to find that one little insight into your situation. Theirs is not an easy job, either. So you have to own a big portion of the work that needs to be done. It is a lot of work. The information is technical and complicated. Research articles are tedious and boring—and often inconclusive. It is not easy for people to process medical information if they don't have a scientific background. But you have to learn the language and understand the disease if you are going to protect yourself.

I do feel that I have one unique advantage over my doctors when we are dealing with scleroderma. Though my doctors have read about scleroderma and have seen scleroderma, I *have* scleroderma. I *feel* scleroderma. There is nothing like firsthand experience with the subject matter when you are trying to understand it.

I realize that I could be so close to scleroderma that I might miss something, misinterpret something, or be biased about something. I do not have the broader comprehensive medical knowledge that my physicians have. That is why we need to work with our doctors and hear their interpretation of the information. But ultimately, you must learn to listen to your own gut because you are the one who will live with the decisions. I am grateful that my physicians work with me and are willing to listen to my opinions even if they have a different point of view.

No one is born with medical knowledge. We learn it by reading, listening, and talking to others. The information is not simple, but its complexity doesn't make it magical. I can appreciate a physician's concern that patients may unnecessarily become frightened or confused by all of the information. Some people may be obsessed or extremely sensitive to symptoms or changes in their bodies and burden the health care system with unnecessary office visits. But physicians also need to learn to work with patients who have increasing access to health information by directing them to reliable sources of information, support groups, or health educators who can support the patients to be well informed and well equipped in making all of the decisions that will be required of them for many years to come.

I came to the first physician in my scleroderma experience with general but distinct symptoms, but he said it wasn't a real problem, discounting me rather than listening to me or pulling a book off a shelf to do a little homework. I found the answer myself in a basic medical textbook from a library. In this case, it was more dangerous for me to be passive and accept his conclusion than to search for answers on my own despite my lack of medical training.

I have only observed one physician actually pull a textbook off his shelf in front of me to try and answer a question I had. I was experiencing bone loss in my lower jaw. I had read some research in medical journals and found that this type of bone loss was thought to occur in up to 30 percent of scleroderma patients. The physician said he had not heard of it among scleroderma patients and wanted to take an X-ray to rule out cancer. Then he did something remarkable. He pulled a book off his shelf and looked in it for an answer. There he confirmed my research suggesting

that this type of atrophy was not uncommon with scleroderma. It was a bittersweet situation. I was so appreciative
of the doctor's small gesture, which felt so respectful of me.
Unfortunately neither the textbook nor the physician could
offer a known solution for my problem, but at least he took
the time to check.

Autoimmune illnesses present a unique challenge for
the healthcare system. The individual with the autoimmune
illness is typically a young adult who otherwise would
have few physical health problems. The traditional healthcare system is inclined to focus on the most life-threatening
aspects of the disease. Of course this is of primary impor-
tance, but it is also important to consider the quality of life
of the whole person. Ironically, the increasing success of the
healthcare system in preventing premature death among
people with autoimmune diseases has opened up a new
challenge: long-term management of people with these
chronic illnesses.

The ongoing symptoms of an autoimmune illness might
not debilitate you, but they will drain you. You might look
normal but you could feel horrible. You will have to learn
to navigate twenty-five to thirty years of health evaluations,
setbacks, medicines, and remissions along with the slow,
creeping damage caused by the disease. It would be easy
to develop a pessimistic mindset that you are just biding
your time, waiting for some disaster to happen. You have to
choose a more proactive and positive mindset if you want to
live your life and protect the health you have.

There is more to health than the tangible, measurable,
reimbursable benchmarks presented by today's healthcare
system. Very early in the development of my scleroderma I

knew something was wrong with my health, but my doctor couldn't measure what I was experiencing so he concluded that there was nothing wrong. But the truth was that he simply didn't know how to measure what I was experiencing.

On the opposite end of my first medical experience with scleroderma, there was a situation in which I felt that I was well but was told by my doctor that I was not. I ignored my feeling of wellness because of my doctor's measurements indicating that I was not well and specifically that my lungs were not functioning adequately. My intuition said that because I was still running three miles daily with no change in how I felt, I should question the pulmonary function measures. My intuition turned out to be right. The pulmonary function test turned out to be a false positive and I was not in any immediate danger. My own experience and intuition had been valid, and it taught me that I had to learn to speak up when I knew a doctor's pronouncement didn't feel right.

Part of advocating for yourself lies in being in charge of how you define yourself. Self-image is influenced by many people and factors outside of yourself, including family, media, role models, and social norms.

Well-meaning but negative comments from others can be hard to deflect. It can be hard to prevent negative, stereotypical, or hopeless comments from sticking to you. I try not to be overly sensitive, but, honestly, I have to make a deliberate effort not to let negative words spin in my mind. The danger in not filtering other people's comments is that these comments can influence how you see yourself and consequently affect what you believe you can or cannot be and do.

Frequently, during my regular medical exams, a medical student participates in the evaluation in order to learn about scleroderma. During one of these visits, my physician introduced me to a medical student and then added, "She is our most optimistic patient. She always thinks she is getting better."

I know my physician did not mean to discount me with this remark, but there was an unfortunate subtle message in that statement. When the physician said, "She always thinks she is getting better," what I heard was, "She thinks she is getting better even though we know she is not."

I know my physician meant nothing negative by this comment. I came to understand, however, that my doctor and I were looking at the idea of "better" in two different ways. I was looking at it in terms of function and feeling. My doctor was looking at it in terms of presence or absence of disease and symptoms.

I felt "better" because I was learning to manage the disease. It is amazing how much better you feel when you can adapt to changes. In the beginning of my experience with scleroderma, I was constantly frustrated by the changes scleroderma was causing and was weighed down by my negative feelings. A large portion of those feelings arose from the uncertainty of how my disease would progress or how to manage the problems that were emerging. I had no perspective or experience to draw from to pace myself or calm myself.

As I learned to adapt to scleroderma, I felt a greater sense of control of my life. My spirits were lifted, my feelings were more positive, and I knew I was "better." My ability to adapt was a key component to my feeling of well-being.

I don't want to trivialize the amount of effort it takes to feel "better" with scleroderma. Anyone who has experienced this disease knows exactly what I mean by this. I write this paragraph with hands that are clearly affected by scleroderma. Despite a big, ugly ulcer on one of my fingers, I spent two hours today working in the yard. I shoveled dirt, spread mulch, and planted shrubs. It's not that I don't have discomfort during these activities, but I've learned to adapt to the pain. The pain is not less than it was in the past, but now it's just expected. It's not always foremost in my mind and it does not keep me from living my life.

Adapting to the pain does not mean I hate it any less. I'm just more familiar with it. I do get frustrated. I do cry. I do get angry. But I am constantly adapting, which lessens the negative feelings. Without even thinking, I use my hands differently in typing, touching, cleaning, bathing. I eat differently, sleep differently, pace myself differently, and choose differently.

As positive as adaptation is generally, though, I've discovered that it can also have downsides. Maybe the biggest downside is the possibility of forgetting yourself a bit and pushing your body to its breaking point. You might forget to appreciate what is important about your adaptations. Or you might allow yourself to drift back into some toxic situations or skip a few of the protective practices that help you to feel "better." It's important to not let yourself be lulled into forgetting how your body has changed and that it needs extra care.

Adapting allows you to create a new "normal." An exercise physiology principle that deals with adaptation states that our bodies will adapt to a consistent challenge as long as the challenge doesn't overwhelm the body. What used to feel hard will eventually feel easier because we are better equipped (anatomically, physiologically, or psychologically) to deal with the challenge. So it "feels" easier even though it is technically just as hard as it ever was.

Scleroderma "feels" easier to me not because I have fewer symptoms or less discomfort but because I have found ways to adapt to the challenges it presents. I do feel like I am "better" than I was when first diagnosed with scleroderma. Seeing myself as "better" is a self-perception and a state of mind I choose to have.

Advocating for yourself also extends into your personal and professional relationships. Setting healthy boundaries to protect yourself from unnecessary stress or energy drains will become a lifelong challenge. Each person with a chronic disease or disability has to negotiate feelings resulting from the physical, emotional, and spiritual changes they experience. You will also have to decide how you will respond to these changes, let go of attachments to the way you have always done things, and be willing to create a new normal. I have found that talking with other people who have scleroderma makes it much easier to advocate for myself. It helps to validate many feelings, challenges, and needs I have. Being able to say, "I feel that, too!" is liberating. It helps me to feel less guilty about asking for assistance or setting limits with others.

Family, friends, and colleagues will be going through their own adjustments as they come to terms with what your illness will mean to them and their relationship with you. I have heard many family members, spouses, and friends express their sadness, frustration, and worries about a loved-one's illness. Some of them feel overwhelmed and helpless. Others feel resentment. Many are loving, generous, and patient. Their perceptions or misconceptions, however, should not dictate your limitations, how you see yourself, or what type of support you need. Like your relationship with your healthcare provider, your relationships with your friends, family, and co-workers should be one of mutual respect. We need their understanding but they need ours as well.

Perhaps the most important advocacy you will do is the advocacy you negotiate with yourself. There is no known cure for scleroderma or lupus or any other autoimmune disease at this time. So you have to play the cards you have been dealt and decide that you are going to live your life as well as possible in spite of your disease. There are some pretty rotten problems that could lie ahead for me with scleroderma. But I try not to dwell on those problems. Why would I ruin a perfectly good day imagining how horrible things could be in the future? You subject yourself to negative feelings even though nothing bad is happening now. I have made a personal commitment to do the best I can to avoid these problems, but quickly remind myself that I am not experiencing those problems today. Appreciate what you have while you have it. You get good at what you practice. Focusing on the present good in your life and embracing a positive, yet realistic outlook about the future is worth practicing. The alternative is to not only suffer the disease but also lose your chance to enjoy the time you have.

Only you can decide what a worthwhile way to live your life is. The Ugly Dress is not your life. It might make some things harder, it might add bumps in the road and shorten the time you have, but you can still have a life with love, joy, inspiration, wonder, gratitude, and beauty. You can still make the world a better place, and make a difference in the lives of others. No one is a better testament of this than a woman I had the great honor to know, Amy Parrish. Amy was our South Carolina Scleroderma Foundation Chapter president who lost her battle with scleroderma in 2010. Amy was a force that seemed unstoppable. Despite tremendous physical suffering, she led the SC Chapter to become a viable statewide organization providing much needed awareness and education to patients, families, and doctors. She was not shy about asking for what she or the SC Chapter needed. She lived every minute of her life even when it seemed impossible to the rest of us. Her strength, determination, and passion showed all of us what could be done if we set our minds to it. She would be the first to say that living with a terrible disease does not mean you cannot have a full and rich life.

Navigating the Healthcare System

Forgive Your Healers

By Karen

MEDICINE HAS MADE such amazing advances in so many areas that we might have unrealistic expectations of what our healthcare providers can do or how long it should take to solve problems. There are also a lot of forces playing a role in how information is interpreted and decisions are made in today's healthcare system.

I have often said that you have to forgive your traditional doctors and alternative healers. Each one has a bias or limitation in the way they analyze or approach a problem. I want to clarify that I dearly love and appreciate my traditional and alternative healthcare providers. I mean no disrespect with my statement. I know my health care providers on both sides of the traditional/alternative divide truly want to help me. But they tend to see things from very different perspectives, and it can be frustrating to go back and forth between the ends of this continuum of care. It often makes me feel like a child of divorced parents. Neither party really speaks well of the other, and they definitely can't communicate with each other for my benefit. Each offers something important but insufficient to my total well-being. I need both of them.

Many people use nontraditional healthcare that is not proven or covered by insurance. I think this reflects an unmet need that patients have within traditional healthcare. In my case, at least, I find that when I have a problem for which no one in the traditional system has a solution, I'm not likely to simply say, "OK, I'll just wait right here until you find a cure." I am not looking for a magical cure from my alternative healers. Instead, I tend to be looking for ways to prevent further damage, to slow the progression of the damage, or to ease the stress that comes with the disease. I am also looking for the promotion of health beyond just physical health. I want my spirit to be healed because I believe it will soften the turmoil going on in my body and improve my quality of life.

I've learned, however, that I cannot assume alternative healers are open-minded. They might just be "different-minded." I once spoke with a traditionally trained physician who moved his practice into an alternative medicine dimension. I told this person that I was exploring alternative health strategies to complement traditional health strategies. I said that I was not expecting a cure, just to minimize the impact of scleroderma and prevent as much damage as possible. I explained that I felt I could be healed without being cured.

He responded by telling me that I had a terrible attitude. He thought I should believe that I could be cured. I was stunned by his response. When I replied that neither he nor anyone else was going to keep me from ultimately getting old and dying of something, he disagreed. Though he presented himself as an alternative healer, his paternalistic style made me uncomfortable. I was almost certain that he would be inclined to tell me what to do rather than working with me to decide what was best for my situation.

Typically, though, I have found that alternative healers address emotional and spiritual healing as well as physical healing. They are more likely to acknowledge the mind-body connection. Building emotional and spiritual health can help to counterbalance the stress of physical disease. My alternative healers typically spend about an hour of time with me during each meeting. The attention, time, and care they give not only help me physically but also help me emotionally and spiritually. Many alternative strategies lack biological feasibility, but some do tap into a powerful dimension of the human mind-body ability that we don't understand very well. It is important to acknowledge that just because we don't understand something, this doesn't mean it doesn't exist or have a beneficial effect. It just means we don't understand it. Drug trials using placebo and control groups regularly find that a considerable number of placebo group participants demonstrate measurable improvement despite being on the placebo. Instead of discounting this phenomenon as a meaningless "placebo effect," we should find out how to tap into the power of the mind to positively impact health outcomes.

There is research to support the existence of positive biological changes associated with alternative therapies like therapeutic touch, massage therapy, and acupuncture therapy. Maybe as important as the modality is the therapeutic benefit that comes with being cared for as a whole person by another person. Of course this is not a feature exclusive to alternative healers. Traditional healers do care for their patients. They are, however, under a tremendous amount of pressure to see as many patients as possible in the least amount of time. They have less time to build the personal bonds that an alternative healer might build with hours of one-on-one time with a single patient.

Unfortunately, some alternative healers' knowledge of physical processes is poor, and many of them have not studied biology, physiology, anatomy, or chemistry. Nor have many of them studied the biochemistry of nutrition or seen the inside of the human body. Consequently, they can be too accepting of what they read and hear in alternative health information sources, over-relying on the stories of individuals as their source of proof that something works. I realize that if a person feels improvement, I am certainly in no position to discount that improvement. But I think we have to be very careful about what we agree to put inside our bodies based on untested alternative recommendations. Though alternative healers might be well-intentioned, not all are well-informed about the risks that various nutrition or supplement interventions could place on people with special physical circumstances, like autoimmune disease. I recognize that I have my own bias about this as a health educator who has studied science and nutrition and some alternative folks might say I am close-minded here. That may be. As the patient, you will have to do your homework to understand the benefits and risks of any intervention in order to protect yourself. This would apply to both alternative and traditional healing strategies.

Traditional healers say that they have to make treatment decisions based on scientific data. However, I think they often have to rely on anecdotal evidence, too, because few large empirical studies look at various drugs or interventions on individuals with autoimmune disease; nor do they look at the interaction of multiple treatments in this population. Traditional medicine tends to rely on prescription medication for prevention and symptom management. Physicians often are not inclined to have much confidence in behavior-change strategies and usually do not recommend specific exercises or changes in diet to help manage stress or other quality-of-life issues associated with autoimmune diseases. While traditional medicine is very skilled at monitoring and managing symptoms through testing, medications, and surgery, it is not as likely to assess emotional or spiritual factors involved with disease. Physical symptom management is very important but it doesn't address many of the other quality-of-life and health promotion practices that can make day-to-day living better.

I can appreciate the traditional physician's apprehension about relying on lifestyle changes to manage symptoms. It's harder to control the "dose" of behavioral or mental health strategies. Patient compliance with diet and physical activity recommendations can be a real challenge. Traditional healers are also restricted to some extent by the insurance industry's very limited support for alternative or behavioral strategies. And, at least for now, health promotion behavior strategies and alternative medicine strategies have not been well studied in the context of their impact on autoimmune illness. However, I think these lifestyle approaches have been too easily overlooked because of their challenges. More attention needs to be given to studying lifestyle management and its role in treating autoimmune diseases.

When you have a chronic illness, your relationships with your various healers will be some of the most important relationships you have in your life. I can't even begin to tell you what peace of mind I have knowing my traditional doctors will be there fighting for me if I have a crisis. I also know my alternative healers will be there to lift my spirit and ease my suffering. So when I say you must forgive your healers, I mean you have to respect where they are coming from just as you want them to respect where you are coming from. It is important to work with someone you feel you can talk to about whatever you need. I once heard that relationships are built one conversation at a time. I encourage you to create the healthcare team that works best for you and build a relationship with them that includes mutual respect and open communication. And though the healthcare system can be a frustrating system to deal with, remember our healers are doing their best to help us be as healthy as possible.

Navigating the Healthcare System

Beware of False Promises

By Linda

W HEN OTHERS LEARNED I had lupus, I was over-whelmed with their well-intentioned claims about a cure for lupus if only I used their particular sup-plement, product, or therapy. Individuals I had never met contacted me and promised that for only so much money a month (often as much as $150 to $200) I could be completely well again!

Because of my medical background, I am very cynical about promised cures. For many serious illnesses, such as lupus or scleroderma, there are not cures, just therapies to help manage them. I'm especially leery of personal testimonies, such as a person or group of people declaring that they once had lupus or some other disease and were "miraculously cured" by taking a particular product or therapy. There is a fundamental flaw in that kind of thinking. Even if one person got better or well after taking the product or therapy, this doesn't mean that the product was what caused the person to improve. It could have happened just by chance, or something else could have happened in the person's life at just about the same time. One person's favorable experience with a product or therapy may have been due to a remission or lull in the disease or from earlier or concurrent use of approved medical treatments.

A wide variety of medical and health practices and products are available that are not generally considered to be part of traditional medicine. They are referred to as Complementary and Alternative Medicine (CAM). Scientific evidence supports some CAM therapies, but for most there are key questions that are yet to be answered through well-designed scientific studies—questions such as whether these therapies are safe and whether they work for the purposes for which they are used.

There is a difference between complementary medicine, which is used together with traditional medicine, and alternative medicine, which is used in place of traditional medicine. An example of a complementary therapy is aromatherapy. An example of an alternative therapy is using a special diet or herbs to treat cancer instead of undergoing surgery, radiation, or chemotherapy that has been recommended by a conventional doctor.

In spite of my skepticism, I believe that it's best to keep an open mind. If there is something out there that can help the lupus or make me more comfortable without harming my body (or my pocketbook), why not?

Over the years, I have tried things like ginger tea because ginger is supposed to have anti-inflammatory properties and lupus is an inflammatory disease. Ginger is cheap, so I have made lots of ginger tea. I can't say that it has helped manage the lupus, but it didn't harm me in any way and may have helped my digestive system. I have also tried fish oil supplements and foods with anti-inflammatory properties (such as blueberries and strawberries). None of these things have "cured" me, but at least I am doing something positive for my overall health.

A complementary therapy that has helped me to relax and feel better is therapeutic touch. Karen has used a therapeutic touch therapist consistently once a month for help with her scleroderma. Therapeutic touch is one of many therapies included in energy medicine, which is based on the concept that human beings are infused with a subtle form of vital energy that is thought to flow throughout the human body. Practitioners of energy medicine believe that illness comes from disturbances of these vital energies. In therapeutic or healing touch, the therapist identifies imbalances of energy in the body and corrects a client's energy by passing his or her hands over the client.

Many small studies of therapeutic touch have suggested its effectiveness for a wide variety of conditions, including wound healing, osteoarthritis, migraine headaches, and anxiety in burn patients. Although there has been little rigorous scientific research to date, according to the National

Center for Complementary and Alternative Medicine, overall these therapies have impressive anecdotal evidence.

When I arrived for my first therapeutic touch session, I was so weak and tired that I sat in my car in the therapist's driveway and cried and prayed before I could go forward. The therapist put me immediately at ease because her presence and the overall ambiance were so calm and serene.

If you've ever had a professional massage, you would recognize the setup for touch therapy as very similar (quiet room with a massage table, soft lighting, and music in the background). I undressed except for bra and panties and then lay on a table with a sheet covering me.

As the therapist's hands moved slowly above my body I could feel the energy movement even though her hands never touched any part of me. She identified several energy imbalances. I can't remember everything she said, but I do recall her noting that fear was keeping a lot of my energy locked in my kidney area. She got it right about the fear. I was definitely afraid (afraid of the illness, afraid of facing life alone, afraid of not being able to do my job because of the sickness and fatigue). She concentrated a lot of her time in the lower-back area, and I could feel tingling as she moved her hands back and forth. I felt more myself when I left the session. Strictly from my personal viewpoint, therapeutic touch is a perfect way to pause, think, reflect, and relax in order to gain strength to move on.

After trying numerous CAM therapies, I have decided that for me, the best approach to managing my lupus is traditional medical care combined with complementary or alternative therapies—if I can afford them and if they have some scientific merit. It's important for anyone to get the facts and be wary and wise about trying any new therapy, and this is especially true for those of us with autoimmune illnesses. There may be risks involved. Be wary of claims such as "natural," "scientific breakthrough," "miracle cure," and "secret ingredient." Many products are advertised as "natural," but that doesn't mean they're safe. Wild mushrooms are natural. Flowers are natural. Some flowers and mushrooms are edible and others are poisonous. Many dietary supplements and herbs have their own side effects or they can interact adversely with prescription or over-the-counter medications.

Talk with your doctor to be certain that a particular CAM therapy or product won't interfere with any traditional treatments or medications you're taking. I've found the National Center for Complementary and Alternative Medicine, http://www.nccam.nih.gov/, to be a reliable source of information. You can also find information about dietary supplements at the website of the Food and Drug Administration, http://www.fda.gov/. If there has been deceptive advertising regarding the therapy and enforcement action has been taken, you may find information at the Federal Trade Commission's website, http://www.ftc.gov/.

Don't be shy about getting second and maybe even third opinions about your diagnosis or about possible treatments, whether the treatments are traditional, complementary, or alternative. Although I liked and trusted my rheumatologist, I had a hard time submitting my body to his recommended treatments, which seemed to be as scary as the disease. I went to three additional rheumatologists in three different states before I reconciled myself to the fact that I indeed have lupus and indeed will probably have to take medications the rest of my life. For someone like me—a nurse who seldom took an aspirin before lupus and who once looked at all medications as potentially poisonous—this was not a cheerful prospect.

I believe the smartest thing you can do after receiving a scary diagnosis or when considering a new therapy is to learn all you can. All the information and different opinions may confuse you at first, but they can be very helpful in the long run.

Pain

By Karen

This pain is relentless.
It reaches in so deep and squeezes and burns.
The healing hurts as much as being injured.
And when it's all over, I'm left exhausted and scarred.
Tired of this pain, should I hope to go numb?
Funny how "not feeling" hurts, too.

Pieces

By Karen

I sift through all of the pieces,
Sorting them into piles;
Thoughts, words, actions.
I want to put it all in order.
Translate it into some sensible message.
There must be some hidden, magical,
prophetic message in all of these pieces.
The pieces define who I am;
Who I want to be;
How people see me;
How I see them.
So many pieces. Some so beautiful,
And others so ugly.
How can I sort them all?

More Pieces

By Karen

I am so tired and angry.
I feel broken to pieces.
I try to keep the pieces together, scraping them into a pile.
But the pile keeps falling apart.
The doctors say "you're really okay . . . because
most of your pieces seem to be in the pile."
They don't see that you are not whole.
They only see you as pieces.
They count them . . . oops! There goes another.
Now let's start over . . . one, two, three.

Faith

By Karen

Details swirl around me like electrons around a nucleus.
I am so close to all of them that I cannot see the whole.
I fear I do not have control and chaos is all around me.
So faith must calm my nervous mind to
believe the truth I cannot see.

Managing Perceptions

Learn Your Hooks

By Linda

MY NIECE, ERIN, was born with a deficiency of cilia in her lungs. Since the cilia couldn't do its job and sweep bacteria and other contaminants up and out of her airways, she had frequent bouts of pneumonia. She also had severe asthma to the degree that she sometimes stopped breathing and my sister would have to do CPR.

Erin had to take large doses of prednisone to calm the inflamed airways. She was a petite and beautiful child with big soulful brown eyes, but the prednisone changed her appearance and gave her the typical prednisone face, round and fat.

She often had to be home-schooled when she was sick, so children at school didn't always see the gradual change in her appearance from the prednisone. I'm sure when she returned to school the children were sometimes surprised by her altered appearance.

After a particularly bad episode of illness, she returned to school and one of the boys said to her, "You sure have gotten ugly." Erin is very intelligent and has a sharp tongue. She quickly retorted, "My ugliness is temporary. Yours is permanent!"

People weren't rude enough to comment on the changes prednisone made in my appearance, although changes were definitely there. My face took on the typical full moon shape. I grew facial hair. Luckily, the hair was blonde and downy and not dark and coarse. The hair on my head thinned. When it grew back, it was curly. I developed a buffalo hump on my back and humps above my clavicles. And of course, after the initial phase of illness when I was so sick that I actually lost weight, I put on lots of extra pounds.

I looked in the mirror and no longer saw myself—I saw someone with lupus. Sometimes when I felt my very worst, people would say, "But you look so good!" Having gone through the experience with my husband where he believed that my illness was all in my mind, I interpreted those comments as, "You don't *look* sick, so you must not be sick!" My response was anger. I usually commented, "Well, I'm grateful I don't look as bad as I feel. Otherwise, I'd be sick and ugly, too."

Other remarks that seemed okay on the surface also carried perceived or nonverbal messages that made me angry. A couple of these mental "hooks" for me went like this: "Do you think it's just stress?" Nonverbal message: "You did this to yourself." Or: "Do you think if you'd just exercise more (eat less wheat, eliminate dairy products, etc.), you'd feel better?" Nonverbal message: "If you'd just try harder, you'd get well."

I heard the remark about exercising more from my twenty-five-year-old son, and I wanted to cry. I heard judgment and accusation in his voice, not loving concern. I knew he had been influenced by his father who believed then and still believes the lupus is all in my head.

It took me a long time to get past the anger at such remarks even though I knew most of them were well-intentioned. One day I realized it was not the actual words that hurt, but the fact that the words touched wounds left by my husband. Getting angry with the people making the remarks was just an excuse for me to get mad. It really had nothing to do with them.

One of the biggest lessons I've learned in my process of healing is to identify my "hooks." A hook is any word or comment that causes you to instantly react in a hostile or defensive way. By allowing another person to "hook" you into a response, you allow yourself to be victimized by others. You make something big out of something little because you have the need to be right and make everybody else wrong. By realizing that people act according to their own belief system and that what they say or do is because they see the world with different eyes, you can begin to learn to stop getting mad. Now when people learn that I have lupus and comment that I look good, I receive the comment gratefully and graciously say, "Thank you."

The following story was sent to me in one of those ubiquitous email blasts, which I usually just delete. This time I read the story and saved it because it demonstrates clearly that perceptions are not reality. They are simply other people's views of the situation, and their viewpoints have been shaped by their own life experiences.

Walking the Dog

Unexpectedly, an airplane was diverted to Sacramento along its route. The flight attendant explained that there would be a delay and if the passengers wanted to get off the aircraft, the plane would reboard in fifty minutes. Everybody got off the plane except one lady who was blind. A man had noticed her as he walked by and could tell the lady was blind because her Seeing Eye dog lay quietly underneath the seats in front of her throughout the entire flight. He could also tell she had flown this very flight before because the pilot approached her and, calling her by name, said, "Kathy, we are in Sacramento for almost an hour. Would you like to get off and stretch your legs?" The blind lady replied, "No thanks, but maybe Buddy would like to stretch his legs." Picture this: All the people in the gate area came to a complete standstill when they looked up and saw the pilot walk off the plane with a Seeing Eye dog! The pilot was even wearing sunglasses. People scattered. They not only tried to change planes, but they were even trying to change airlines!

Managing Perceptions
Avoid Being Labeled

By Linda

I WAS AT LUNCH one day with a nursing colleague. We talked about family, work, friends, and other topics and then she asked, "Aren't you an ACOA?" I didn't know at first what she was talking about, but after a moment I recognized the acronym for Adult Child of an Alcoholic. I paused for a moment and said, "Yes, my father was an alcoholic."

I didn't say this to her at the time, but it's what I believed then and still believe: My father's alcoholism strongly influenced the person I've become. Lupus has strongly influenced the person I've become. And many other events in my life have also influenced me. However, I'm more than an ACOA or a lupus patient. I'm much too complex to be summed up in a label.

Dr. Carolyn Myss, in her book *Why People Don't Heal and How They Can,* says that during her travels she meets some people who seem to define themselves by their wounds. These individuals cling to labels such as "adult child of an alcoholic" or "incest survivor" as badges of courage. She describes this attitude as "woundology" and says that people around the world are confusing the healing value of self-expression with permission to manipulate others with their wounds. Instead of viewing the uncovering of their wounds as an early stage of the healing process, they continue to use them to manipulate others.

Dr. Myss describes a woman who, upon introduction to a new person, would begin by explaining that in order to become friends with her, the other person would have to honor her wounds. This woman went on to say that she had experienced many wounds in her childhood and that during her healing process she was likely to have mood swings. She expected others to respect, not challenge, her swings. She expected her support system to adjust their moods to hers and not joke or laugh around her.

Dr. Steven Wolin, a psychiatrist, in a speech to members of the American Association for Marriage and Family Therapy, said that America is being turned into a nation of emotional cripples. As a culture, we are glorifying frailty, lumping trivial disappointments with serious forms of mental illness, and portraying the human condition as a disease. Instead, he believes, we should focus on the human capacity to rise above adversity and develop lasting strengths while doing so.

Part of becoming a mature person is to discover and understand who you are, what you want your life to mean, and to love yourself. It also means recognizing that although you may have been influenced by what has happened in your life, you are not exclusively any of those things. My ex-husband often tried to label me by saying such things as, "you're selfish," "you are a glass half-empty kind of person," or "you're just like your mother." (He disliked my mother intensely because he thought she was too controlling.) My response was always, "Yes, I can act selfishly at times. Yes, I can sometimes look at the glass as half-empty. Yes, I can sometimes be bossy and controlling. However, I'm not *exclusively* any of those things!"

Labels and models are used often in our society to identify and classify things so that they can be more easily understood. The dictionary describes a label as "a way of identifying or classifying something" and a model as a "schematic description of a system, theory, or phenomenon that accounts for its known or inferred properties and may be used for further study of its characteristics."

While I was attending a healthcare executive program at UCLA, one of my professors said that all models are wrong but some models are useful. Models are *useful* because they present complex information in an understandable manner. Models are *wrong* because they present complex information in an understandable manner. In trying to simplify a complex situation, a model doesn't address all the nuances and subtleties.

I believe labels have the same inherent problem as models. Just as complex things cannot be summed up completely by a model, human beings can't be summed up in a label. I don't want to be seen exclusively as a sick person or a lupus patient. I prefer to be seen as a whole person, a person who has experienced illness and other difficulties but who has faced those difficulties with grace and has learned more about herself and grown in the process.

Achieving Overall Health and Well-being

Manage Your Thoughts—
Manage Your Life

By Karen

CONSISTENT MESSAGE IN the spiritual material I have read is that to change your life, you must change your thoughts. A well-known Buddhist teaching that comes to mind is:

> *The thought manifests as the word;*
> *The word manifests as the deed;*
> *The deed develops into habit;*

And habit hardens into character;
So watch the thought and its ways with care, and let it
spring from love born out of concern for all beings . . .
As the shadow follows the body, as we think . . . so we become.

For me, living well in spite of disease comes down to understanding and managing my thoughts. How will I behave in response to my thoughts? As the proverb suggests, thoughts are the root of our habits. Habits of thought and habits of behavior go hand in hand.

I can never scientifically prove that my worried thoughts and anxiety about "doing things right" or "living up to someone else's expectations" were the catalysts causing my immune system to literally "run amok" on my body. But I know it in my gut. I know it every time my worries rise up and dominate my thoughts, and I begin to feel the heat in my forearms and the tightness in my hands and face and the swelling in my feet. I don't have to wait for years to see the price that my worries are costing me. I can see it in a few days—sometimes in a few minutes.

An individual I have worked with made an offhanded statement to me once that new faculty have to be willing to make sacrifices to "make it" in academe. I responded by saying that the word *sacrifice* was too abstract. No one really thought about what was being asked of the new faculty members, and faculty members did not really know what they were giving up. So I challenged him to give me an example of what he meant by the word sacrifice. Then I offered my definition of sacrifice by saying, "When you ask me to make a sacrifice, I'm going to ask you, 'Just how much of my finger are we talking about? A quarter of my finger? Half of my finger? The whole finger?' Because when we talk sacrifice, we are talking about living an unhealthy life that will cost me in inflammation, ulceration, pain, and ultimately the loss of portions of my fingers—or worse. So how much 'sacrifice' are you really asking from me?"

I realize that some people might think I was being obnoxious, but frankly, I can't worry about someone who is upset by my disagreeing with the status quo. I'm the one who has to live with the mutilated fingers and the scarred lungs. And for what are we being asked to make such sacrifices? Often we are being asked to make these sacrifices for symbolic accomplishments that mean nothing in the bigger scheme of things. Am I supposed to sacrifice the equivalent of a finger or two because someone else believes that others are only valuable if they can say they published a certain number of research articles or acquired so many dollars in funding? Am I going to perpetuate the myth to my young students that trading your health (physical, social, and mental) for a materialistic accomplishment is somehow noble and honorable?

When we discuss what is asked of most people in exchange for career advancement, we are not talking about making a sacrifice to rescue someone from a burning building or to feed the hungry. Instead, the sacrifices most of us are asked to make are for the sake of *claiming* a number of some kind or appearing to have achieved some status. Is such status, individually or for the sake of an organization's goals, worth even one fingertip?

I believe that we have to do a better job helping people understand what they are tangibly "sacrificing" when they engage in many socially accepted and respected kinds of thoughts and actions so they can at least make informed choices. We have to begin by helping people to reexamine their thoughts to determine if these are hardening into habits that doom them to unhealthy, unhappy, imbalanced lives—regardless of whether they have an autoimmune disease or not.

People are metaphorically trading their fingertips for symbolic accomplishments every day. They just don't see that this is what they are doing because it can take a long time to see the damage—but the damage is being done nonetheless. Physical damage might be the easiest to observe, but it could just as easily be social damage, emotional damage, or spiritual damage.

It is hard to turn down the rewards society hands out—money, prestige, acknowledgments, and praise. We are trained early in life to strive to accomplish things, and we are rewarded with approval, gold stars, grades, and money. I have been conditioned just like everyone else to do what is right, be my best, and try to excel in what I do. But too often we do these things to meet the expectations of others who are telling us what we should do and who we should be.

I don't believe you can really be happy when you believe your worth is dependent on someone else's judgment of you. I don't know if any of us can ever be completely free of the influence of external judgments. I know I am not completely free of it. But I believe that to be happy, I have to become strong enough to endure the comments from others that more or different things were expected from me. You have to be able to stand calmly while being compared to others.

To not be a disappointment to myself, I might have to be willing to be a disappointment to others.

When I was a teenager, my father told me about the Gestalt Prayer:

> *I am I and you are you.*
> *I was not put on this earth to live up to your expectations and you were not put here to live up to mine.*
> *And if by chance we meet, that is wonderful.*
> *If not, it can't be helped.*
> *If by chance what makes me happy makes others happy, that is wonderful. If not, it can't be helped.*

Those other people are going to have to learn to live with their disappointment in me. All joking aside, it is a constant struggle to manage thoughts that have been so long molded to seek outside approval.

In some odd and ironic way, scleroderma has forced me to see things in a different way and perhaps increase my level of true happiness—not measured in appearance, dollars, awards, or publications, but in calmer thoughts and stronger gratitude for what I have. Scleroderma is helping to teach me that my attention needs to be on positive thoughts and my internal values rather than negative thoughts and external judgments. What a sad waste of time it would be to spend the short time that I have on this earth fixated on what I don't have or what is not perfect in my life.

Achieving Overall Health and Well-being

Laugh Out Loud (LOL)

By Linda

𝓘'M SURE YOU'VE all heard the lines, "Laugh and the world laughs with you. Weep and you weep alone." I realized the truth of this one day while working as a nurse. I had experienced a particularly difficult day, and when one of the doctors asked casually, "How are you?" I responded with, "Do you want me to lie or tell the truth?" He replied, "Lie. I get paid for the truth."

Most of us agree that it is more enjoyable to be with people who have a sense of humor and the ability to laugh at life than those who constantly bemoan their circumstances. Being around negative people, particularly those who believe they have no power to change things in their lives, can increase your stress level and may make you doubt your ability to manage stress in healthy ways.

Humor can be a healthy way of distancing yourself from problems, allowing you to step away and look at your problems with perspective. Laughter triggers a release of tension and may even provide therapeutic benefits. Research regarding the health benefits of laughter is limited and it's difficult to prove cause and effect. Studying laughter's potential health benefits began twenty years ago when Norman Cousins, in *Anatomy of an Illness*, told his story of overcoming a fatal disease by watching old Charlie Chaplin movies. He said that laughter is a great antidote to illness.

There has been some recent evidence suggesting laughter may create physiological changes that help maintain health. In study results released in 2000 by the University of Maryland Medical Center, researchers compared the humor responses of three hundred people. Half of the participants had either suffered a heart attack or undergone coronary artery bypass surgery. The other half did not have heart disease. One questionnaire had a series of multiple-choice questions to find out how much or how little people laughed in certain situations. The second questionnaire used true or false questions to measure anger and hostility.

Michael Miller, MD, director of the Center for Preventive Cardiology at the University of Maryland Medical Center and a professor of medicine at the University of Maryland School of Medicine, said the most significant finding from this study was that people with heart disease responded with less humor to everyday life situations. They generally laughed less, even in positive situations, and they displayed more anger and hostility. He also stated that the ability to laugh—either naturally or as learned behavior—may have important implications in societies such as the U.S. where heart disease remains the number one killer.

A second research study on laughter by Dr. Miller and colleagues was presented at the Scientific Session of the American College of Cardiology in 2005. The study used a group of twenty nonsmoking healthy volunteers (equal numbers of men and women). All participants had normal blood pressure, cholesterol, and blood glucose levels. They were randomly assigned to watch a segment of a movie that would cause mental stress or a segment of a movie that would cause laughter. A minimum of forty-eight hours later, they watched the segment of the movie with the opposite effect.

The researchers measured changes in blood vessel reactivity during and after the movies. There were no differences in blood vessel dilation in either the mental stress or laughter phases *during* the movies. However, after the movies were seen, there were striking differences. Beneficial blood vessel relaxation, or vasodilatation, was increased in nineteen of the twenty volunteers after they watched the movie segments that provoked laughter. Even though the study involved a small number of participants, Dr. Miller stated that results seem to strengthen the connection between laughter and cardiovascular health.

In another study, Lee S. Berk of Loma Linda University and Stanley Tan, MD, of the Oak Crest Health Research Institute randomly divided a group of twenty diabetics with high blood pressure and hyperlipidemia into two groups. One group was provided standard care for their medical conditions. The second group received standard care plus thirty minutes of self-selected humor every day.

Participants in the laughter group had higher levels of HDL (high density lipoprotein, the "good" cholesterol) after two months of treatment. After four months they also had decreased levels of substances that cause inflammation (tumor necrosis factor-alpha, interferon-gamma, interleukin-6 and high-sensitivity C-reactive protein). The investigators noted that these changes also made the laughter group participants at lower risk, statistically, for cardiovascular disease associated with diabetes mellitus and the metabolic syndrome.

According to Dr. Robert R. Provine, professor of psychology and assistant director of the Neuroscience Program at the University of Maryland, Baltimore County, definitive research into the potential health benefits of laughter hasn't been done yet. He suggests that what we currently speculate are the benefits of laughter may have more to do with social relationships. Laughter is contagious and may bring people together.

Whatever the research concludes about the health effects of humor and laughter, I believe laughter makes life worth living. Besides, it's free and has no negative side effects. In my family of origin, we have always been able to come up with a funny line even in the direst circumstances. For example, my mother is now eighty-nine and in a nursing home. She has severe congestive heart failure and has knocked at death's door so many times we've lost count. My husband and I visited her one day after a particularly bad episode.

Mother said, "Well, I thought I was really going to see Jesus this time!"

My husband asked, "Mrs. Reeves, do you want to be an angel?"

She looked at him with her characteristic grin and replied, "I don't know. What do angels actually *do*?"

Karen and I joke and laugh our way through many difficult days with our illnesses. As Karen stated at the beginning, "I'll be damned if I'll be stuck with scleroderma *and* a bad attitude!" It's a good idea to give yourself permission to smile or laugh, especially during difficult times. Try to take yourself and life less seriously, and seek humor in everyday happenings. When you can laugh at life, you will feel less stressed and you'll be better able to manage your illness. Think about the man who was mauled by a tiger. As he was being prepped for surgery, the anesthesiologist leaned over and asked him if he was allergic to anything. The man replied, "Yeah, tigers!"

Achieving Overall Health and Well-being

Pamper the Princess

By Linda

a FRIEND OF MINE was at the beach one afternoon when she saw a barefoot little girl dressed in a pink tutu running joyfully about and dashing in and out of the water while an older woman, whom my friend assumed was the grandmother, trudged behind carrying the little girl's shoes and various other things.

My friend said, "I bet she's a little princess."

The grandmother replied, "Yes, but trust me, you do not want to be in her kingdom!"

When I advise you to pamper your inner princess, I am not advocating that you become a spoiled, lazy princess who is imperious and inconsiderate of others. However, I believe that each of us has an inner princess that needs pampering, and we often neglect that princess in the care and nurturing of others.

Why is it that as women we feel selfish and guilty when we take care of ourselves instead of others? When I was at my sickest with lupus and felt at times that I could barely stand, I found myself getting up from rest as soon as I heard my husband's car pull into the driveway. I knew that even though he might not say anything, his judgmental smirk needed no words. The implied message was, "Lying down again, huh? You're not sick. It's all in your head."

So I continued to take care of my husband and son, despite my illness, even after I'd worked all day. Each night I prepared a full and nutritious dinner no matter how bad I felt. One night I was particularly tired. After dinner I told my son that I was not feeling well and asked him to please take his dishes to the sink when he left the table. He did. My husband then carried his dishes to the sink (definitely not a habit of his). He looked at me with his familiar smirk and said, "Well, you've finally gotten what you've wanted all along—a husband and son who do dishes." That was a sign! You teach people how to treat you. I realized I had taught my family to disrespect me by not considering my needs.

In order to get well or to better live with the lupus, I knew that I would have to teach my family and others that I have needs too, and I would have to expect them to respect my needs. You can learn to pamper your internal princess as I did by understanding and setting reasonable and flexible boundaries, and by claiming and celebrating your self-worth.

Understanding and Setting Reasonable and Flexible Boundaries

A lot of people think that if you focus on yourself, it's narcissistic. However, narcissism, in the sense of focusing on yourself and getting your needs met, can be healthy or unhealthy.

Healthy narcissism means that without hurting anyone else, you care for your wants and needs in your own way and in your own time by setting healthy boundaries. Healthy boundaries help you meet needs such as time and space to be alone and to rest when you're tired. Healthy boundaries also help separate what is your responsibility from the responsibility of others. You are responsible for becoming aware of your innermost thoughts and feelings, and you are responsible for your behaviors. You also have the responsibility to make your life successful and joyful. But you are not responsible for the behavior of other people or making others happy and successful.

In Dr. Charles Whitfield's book *Boundaries and Relationships; Knowing, Protecting, and Enjoying the Self,* he describes unhealthy boundaries as those that are set by other or others. He points out that these are often hurtful or harmful, and they may frequently be used as a means of control or manipulation. As you might guess, he says that unhealthy boundaries often build impenetrable walls in relationships.

One way to think about boundaries is to think about the role of cells in your body. Each cell has a wall that keeps it separate from other cells. The cell wall is semi-permeable, which means it lets some things in and out but not others. For example, the cell wall keeps out things that are harmful to the cell, but it allows in helpful things such as nutrients.

Being aware of your boundaries helps you decide who to let into your life and who to keep out. It makes it easy to say "yes" or "no" appropriately. Setting healthy boundaries helps free you to be yourself and to be more comfortable in all of your relationships, especially your closest ones.

We usually learn boundaries in our family of origin, but if you grew up in an unhealthy family as I did, you were never taught to have a healthy self with healthy boundaries. My alcoholic father was very gentle and kind when sober but mean and violent when drunk. He was a long-distance trucker and was away for long periods of time. I was relaxed when he was gone, but on the nights he was expected home, I cringed in my bed and prayed that he would be sober or that he wouldn't come home at all. Too many nights, I awakened to the sounds of loud noises, cursing, furniture knocked over, or the telephone ripped from the wall so we couldn't call the police.

As I mentioned earlier, I felt responsible for the safety of my younger sisters and brother. I usually shepherded them to Miss Lucille's room. She was an elderly woman who rented a room from us. I huddled there with my sisters and brother, listening to Miss Lucille's reassuring words until things settled down.

My dad never harmed us children but he took his rage out on our mother, and I lived with the terror that one day he would kill her. When I was about ten years old, he pulled a knife on Mother and I fought back. I hit him on the back with an iron skillet. I don't think I hit hard enough to hurt him much, but it was hard enough to call him to his senses.

As a result of the violence in my family of origin, I learned to hate heated arguments and conflict of any kind. When I married, I was determined to have a good marriage and to create a calm and nurturing environment for my family. In retrospect, I failed to set boundaries to protect my well-being and to limit how much I tolerated before saying, "Ouch, you hurt me!" in response to the verbal and emotional hurts that I felt. Many times, for example, I felt an encroachment of my sense of right and wrong, a basic lack of fairness about the way my husband treated me, especially related to the division of chores in the home. I talked to him many times about how I felt, but he chose not to understand. He was trained as a military pilot, and his paradigm of marriage was simple: "I'm the pilot. You're the copilot. I lead, you follow." He believed that a man should not have to do anything related to housework even if the woman had worked twelve hours to his eight and was sick with a serious disease.

My boundaries were loose and ill-defined. I allowed my husband's scorn to keep me from getting the rest that my body desperately needed. I allowed him to constantly put me down and tell me what I thought and how I felt. He continuously told me that I was unhappy even though I didn't *feel* unhappy. In retrospect, it's so easy to see how arrogant it was of him to think he knew better than I what I felt. In contrast to my boundaries that were loose and ill-defined, my husband's boundaries were rigid and inflexible, probably because of issues with his own family of origin.

I now know that a boundary that is too rigid often masks hostility or mistrust. When I was hospitalized with lupus, he built a wall around himself that I couldn't enter, and he kept it up after I returned home. I knew from past experience that I would waste a lot of energy trying to beat down his wall. I tried, nonetheless, but the wall was impenetrable and I finally gave up.

In the poem "Mending Wall," Robert Frost says that before he built a wall, he'd ask himself who he was walling in or walling out. Healthy boundaries should be strong enough to keep out harmful activities and people but they should be flexible enough to allow in activities and people that nourish and enrich your life.

Claiming and Celebrating Your Self-Worth

When my husband decided to divorce me, I was my most unattractive! I had always been considered slim and pretty, but the lupus and large doses of intravenous steroids followed by months of high-dose oral steroids had stolen the face and the figure I once knew. When I looked in the mirror, I saw a bloated old woman.

Every day, I found another surprise somewhere on my body—bruises, facial hair, thinning patches of hair on my scalp. I felt ugly, and because my husband of twenty-eight years had dumped me, I felt even more so. I wrote in my journal, "I feel thrown away—a thing of no value, like a used tissue."

Fortunately, I realized the devastating effects negative self-talk could have on my self-esteem. I believe that what you say to yourself can become a self-fulfilling prophesy. I caught myself saying repeatedly during the early phase of my illness, "I'm scared to death." One day I realized the enormity of those words and I quit saying them.

Words we say to ourselves influence the way we feel, think, and act. Once said, the words don't die. They stay in our bodies and can cause us to be happy and hopeful or sad, depressed, mean, and maybe even sick.

I decided to stop thinking or referring to myself as a used tissue. Instead, I chose to think of myself as very much like a valuable painting that was hidden away in an attic for many years. Someone cleaning the attic may have perceived the painting as junk and tossed it out, but many others are able to see the painting as beautiful and recognize its inherent value.

One day I read about a woman who was trying to survive the rejection and lowered self-esteem of divorce. She decided to have a special chain made to wear around her waist. She designed a gold medallion to hang from the chain and had it inscribed with the word "Priceless." I joked with my adult son that since I couldn't afford the chain and gold medallion, I was going to get a small tattoo with that same inscription. (He sported at least one tattoo at the time.) I asked him if getting a tattoo would hurt. He smiled and said, "Actually, Mom, I think you'd find it rather liberating!"

I opted instead to design a ring for myself with the word "priceless" inscribed. The ring is a visible and constant reminder that even though I was not valued by my husband, I will never again let my sense of worth be determined by someone else. I have always been and will always be price-less—and so are you!

Taking care of yourself by recognizing and pampering

your inner princess is a healthy thing to do. If you constantly give to others without first taking care of yourself,
you will be totally drained and end up with only bitterness
and resentment. It's important to remind yourself that you
are valued and valuable just as you are. Once you begin
to value yourself, you'll be ready to discover and pamper
your inner princess by setting healthy boundaries and celebrating your self-worth.

Achieving Overall Health and Well-being

Create a Sanctuary

By Karen

WHETHER OR NOT you have a chronic illness, I think it's difficult to preserve your sanity or maintain your priorities today without a personal sanctuary of some kind. In fact, these two words, sanity and sanctuary, are cousins. Sanity describes a sound, healthy mind. One synonym for the word "sane" is "wise." Sanctuary describes a holy place, a place of refuge and protection.

A personal sanctuary provides you with a safe place to invest in your wisdom and well-being. What makes a place a sanctuary for you will be determined by the feeling you get when you are there.

As a child, I remember being drawn to quiet places where I could look out into nature or could be by myself. I needed the solitude to think, imagine, create, and be calm. Sometimes my sanctuary was a secluded section of my family's yard that looked out on a wooded lot beside our house. If I couldn't be outside, I could create a sanctuary by being in my bedroom and listening to music, painting, writing in my journal, or looking out the window. As an adult, I have created sanctuaries throughout my home. And just as when I was a child, I try to create a feeling of happiness that comes from being in the presence of beauty, nature, and order.

My sanctuaries ultimately bring me calmness, happiness, sanity, and wisdom. At times, something as simple as taking a long walk in the woods or sitting on the porch with my dog in my lap gives me a sense of sanctuary. I often feel I'm in a sanctuary when driving long distances in my car as well. If I am alone and drive in silence or with beautiful music playing, I am transported into my mind to think, sort out priorities, and remind myself of who I am.

Although a feeling of sanctuary can be dramatically affected by physical surroundings, a sanctuary doesn't need to be a designated physical place. For me, sanctuary is achieved anywhere I feel safe to engage in quiet thinking or creative expression. There's certainly no reason to think of having a personal sanctuary as a luxury any more than we should think of wisdom, health, and happiness as luxuries. A sense of sanctuary should simply be a regular part of our everyday lives.

For several years, I have been reading about a new area

of research called "positive psychology." Scientists in this field study the concept of happiness and how people can cultivate happiness in life. It's becoming clear that we can cultivate happiness by focusing on our personal strengths (as opposed to giving our attention to our weaknesses), practicing thoughts of gratitude, and engaging in activities that give us a feeling of purpose.

Unfortunately it is a normal part of our culture to place a high value on money, things, status, and physical attributes—qualities we'll sacrifice our health for because we think they will bring us happiness. Of course we all need enough money and material things to feel safe and secure. But the research on happiness reveals that after a certain point, money and things do not provide lasting happiness—only temporary, superficial feelings of pleasure that are mistaken for authentic happiness but quickly disappear.

So we work harder, collect more stuff, and hope that soon we will feel happy. But happiness doesn't come, or if it does, it is only fleeting. Having a place of sanctuary in your life can help you to step outside of the endless busy-ness of modern life, check on your true happiness status, and gauge what you really need to do to be sane (wise).

Achieving Overall Health and Well-being

Redefine "Health"

By Karen

I F YOU ARE living with a serious chronic illness, you will spend the better part of your adult life, as Linda and I have, managing the physical chaos and the spiritual, emotional, and social fallout that come with illness. To do so, consider reexamining what "health" actually means to you. Is it the absence of disease? Is any symptom of disease an unhealthy state? How many symptoms must you have before you label yourself unhealthy? Can you be healthy in spite of your disease?

How you will pursue health and well-being is a very personal journey. It can be as complicated or as simple as you decide to make it. Some people feel their health, while others only feel its absence. Definitions of health and frameworks to measure health have evolved over time. As a nation, we moved our primary health focus from communicable diseases to chronic diseases over the past century. Communicable diseases were combated with waste management and immunizations, and chronic diseases were combated with lifestyle, surgical, and pharmaceutical interventions. During both of these eras, the emphasis was on disease identification, reduction, and management; and significant advances were made in all of these areas.

In a 2006 article in the *American Journal of Public Health,* Dr. Lester Breslow proposed that we are now beginning a new era of how we define health, which he calls the Fruitful Living Era. In this next era, according to Breslow, the way health is viewed will shift from that of "avoiding disease" to one of "maximizing health." This new health era invites us to view health as a resource that allows us to do things we want to do. Health is considered a means rather than an end, a resource for living. The goal is not to achieve a particular health status but to have a long life during which you function well and maximize your potential for living.

As a health professional, I thought I had a good understanding of health. I did all the things I was supposed to, including eating the right foods, not smoking, and remaining physically active. The last thing I worried about was being unhealthy. But I should have been worrying because I was, in the truest sense, living an unhealthy life.

I was unhealthy because I was out of balance. I relied too much on my physical fitness, assuming it alone meant I was healthy. I mistook physical health for total health. It wasn't until I lost my physical health that I could really see how unhealthy I was. I had essentially ignored the other dimensions of my health and allowed them to become weak.

For many years, I had taught others that health is multifaceted and that no one component is more important than another. However, I realize now that I really had a blinding bias towards physical aspects of health. The other health components—spiritual, social, emotional, and mental—were not things I addressed directly in my life. Scleroderma forced me to consider a new definition of health that is much more in keeping with what Dr. Breslow described in his article.

After my scleroderma diagnosis, I struggled to understand why this was happening to me and to recapture physical health. For a short while I focused solely on the absence of physical health and bargained with God to not let my illness get worse. But eventually, between the bargaining and the passing of time, I began to forget what it felt like to be free of disease. I realized that I would probably not be the same physically even if I were to be "cured." Only then did I begin to grapple with all the other pieces of myself, pieces that had been largely ignored because of my preoccupation with my physical self.

Initially, I hoped that if I was a "good girl," took my medicine, and didn't expect too much, I would be rewarded with the return of my physical self as I once knew it, both in terms of appearance and fitness. Of course, that never happened, so I began to look at other ways to give my life meaning and shape my identity. I wanted something to feel happy about. I wanted peace of mind. Slowly I began to realize that I could be healthy in spite of physical "dis-ease." I began to invest in the other areas of my health and consequently was able to decrease the drag that my physical disease had on my overall happiness. I learned to reframe my definition of health in the context of feelings of happiness.

In order to reframe my definition of health, I worked with a life coach to examine the way I thought about myself, my health, and my fears about my future. My life coach helped me to gain clarity about my identity and values beyond my physical health. What was important to me? What did I want my life to look like? How did I want to feel on a daily basis? These questions and many others guided me to a new and more optimistic perspective. I learned that, for me, happiness comes through an appreciation of a few simple pleasures and a sense of purpose. I am happy when I get to learn new things, create new things, and witness beauty. I am happy when I get to spend time with friends and time in nature. I am happy if I think I'm making a valuable contribution to someone in some way.

Scleroderma does not keep me from having these things in my life. My happiness comes from the friendships that social health gives me as well as the loving relationships that emotional health gives me. Spiritual health allows me to feel gratitude for my life and a sense of purpose. And physical health lets me participate in this life and have the energy to do the things I enjoy. Physical health is not an end but a means to other ends, including happiness, maximizing function, and a high quality of life. It is just one part of your total well-being.

Achieving Overall Health and Well-being

Move Your *Buts*

By Karen

UST AS IT'S important to avoid limiting your defini-tion of health solely on your physical health, it's also critical to recognize that you can't afford to forget about it either. Regardless of how limited your physical capacity has become as a result of your disease, you still have the option of being at the high end or the low end of your physical potential. There is a continuous interrelation-ship between diet, exercise, physical health, and chronic disease. Your habits of eating and movement can play an important role in buffering your body against the wear and tear of your autoimmune disease as well as adding to your overall quality of life.

We all have a list of reasons (spoken and unspoken) to explain why we don't eat the right foods and don't get enough physical activity. I would exercise *but* I'm just too tired all the time. I would eat less fast food *but* I don't have time to cook. I know I'm overweight *but* . . . Most of us struggle with choices in today's culture of convenience and plenty, and we can all find lots of excuses to not make healthy choices. But if you have an autoimmune disease or other serious chronic illness, you've probably already discovered that you simply cannot afford to live with unhealthy choices. You have to move your *buts*—all those handy excuses—out of your way. You don't have to be perfect or obnoxious about living a wellness lifestyle, but you do have to make a commitment to prioritize your health. Physical activity and healthy eating are as important as the drugs you take to ward off complications and manage your disease.

Movement as Medicine

I have been very fortunate in my experience with scleroderma to not have the severe and rapid onset of symptoms that can lead to premature death. I attribute a lot of my good fortune to physical activity. Physical activity has always had a soothing and healing effect on me, even before scleroderma. When I am able to be physically active on a regular basis my symptoms are less severe and my feeling of well-being is high. Movement is good medicine for humans. An emerging area within healthcare known as "Exercise as

Medicine" (http://exerciseismedicine.org/) is encouraging physicians to recommend physical activity to their patients for its general health benefits and to help prevent and manage chronic disease. The American College of Sports Medicine also provides guidance to health professionals working with people with chronic diseases and disabilities (Durstine and Moore, 2003) with the goal of optimizing their functional capacity.

There is little research available; however, concerning what is safe and effective exercise for those of us with auto-immune diseases. Because there can be considerable variability in illness severity and symptoms within a given disease, it is impossible to give a one-size-fits-all exercise plan to people managing autoimmune diseases. If we encourage movement rather than exercise, however, I think we can encourage people to pursue physical activity at whatever level is reasonable and healthful for them.

Because of the wide range of challenges you might encounter with an autoimmune disease, you will need to be flexible about your physical activity plan. There could be times when you find that the best movement for you is to get out of your chair and walk around the house for five minutes every hour, or you might find that you can walk briskly for an hour every day. The most important thing is to do what you can when you can, and avoid being motionless the entire day.

Unfortunately, when a disease makes it difficult to move or induces extreme fatigue, you tend to move less and your body becomes weaker and weaker. Everyday activities become harder not only because you have an autoimmune disease but also because your body has gotten out of condition. Still, it's important to find which movements and activities work for you, no matter how simple, and make a commitment to incorporate them into your daily life.

The Best Exercise Is the One You Can—and Will—Do

When I was studying exercise science in college, one of my instructors said that the best exercise is the one you will do. His point was that even if one particular exercise, say cross-country skiing, is scientifically the "best" at meeting cardiovascular health outcomes, it is of no use to you if you dislike cross-country skiing or you won't do it consistently. To be the "best exercise" for you, the activity must be fun and doable. Consistently engaging in an activity you enjoy will be the best exercise for you and will optimize your positive health outcomes. Don't underestimate the value of small doses of activity done consistently. If you engage in a little more activity today than you did yesterday, your body will be healthier.

You'll want to consider several fitness factors as you think about maintaining and enhancing your own physical health: muscle strength and endurance, heart endurance, joint flexibility, and healthy body weight. You don't have to pursue any of these factors at the level of a competitive athlete to gain health benefits. You'll want to work on muscle strength and flexibility to the extent that they allow you to maintain good posture, do the activities you need to do during the day (carry groceries, lift your child, climb stairs, do yard work, or even walk around your house or from the parking lot into your workplace), and participate in recreation that is important to you. You need enough heart endurance that you decrease your risk of high blood pressure, stroke, and heart disease and increase your ability to enjoy walks, dancing, biking, gardening, or whatever you do for fun. We will talk more about body weight later.

Balance Intensity, Duration, and Frequency of Activity

The benefits of physical activity increase as you exercise longer, more frequently, and harder. For heart-health benefits, you need to engage in moderate activity for about thirty minutes (even if it is in three ten-minute sessions) most days of the week. This will amount to about 150 minutes a week. The harder you exercise (vigorous exercise instead of moderate exercise), the less time you need to spend to get the heart-health benefits.

If you are trying to lose weight, exercising for longer periods of time at a moderate level allows you to expend more calories and decrease fat stores. Walking at a moderate pace for sixty to ninety minutes each day is recommended to achieve weight loss goals. If you are trying to bring your stress levels down, the slow, rhythmic movements of yoga and tai chi have been found to have a positive effect on stress hormones. If you are trying to decrease your risk of osteoporosis, weight-bearing activities like walking and running are important.

As these examples emphasize, many of the recommendations we hear regarding physical activity are very specific to particular health goals. Whatever your goals might be, if you have a chronic illness, it's especially important for you to discuss these with your health care provider and determine what activity plan is best for you.

Know Your Turning Point

For everyone, even the elite athlete, there is a point at which increasing the amount you exercise can be harmful. If you are managing a chronic illness, vigorous exercise can lead to greater risk of injury and can place a greater tax on energy reserves. Having an autoimmune disease means you will have to pay careful attention to that turning point. You have to be careful not to trigger a negative immune response with extreme exercise and unintentionally cause excessive inflammation in the working tissues. You must learn your individual turning point — the point at which you are making things worse rather than better with physical activity.

There is no single definition that defines when exercise is "too extreme" for a person with an autoimmune disease. It will vary from person to person and through the course of your life. I was an avid runner when I developed scleroderma and was able to continue running five to six miles at a time for years after the diagnosis. Over time, however, I have had to make adjustments. I learned what types of exercise were right for me through trial and error. I listened to my body and adjusted my running pace to a comfortable level. Eventually, I quit running outside in the winter because my hands and feet could not maintain their circulation. An unexpected possible benefit of this was that I no longer developed bronchitis each winter. I don't know if this health change was a consequence of eliminating cold weather exercise, but if my hands and feet were having difficulty with the cold, it is possible my lung tissue was too.

The point is that it is important to listen to your body. If the activity causes inflammation, makes you feel bad, or makes any of your symptoms worse, you should back off and reexamine your plan. As I tell my own students, anyone can exercise in a way that makes them feel like "crap." The real goal for exercise should be a feeling of rejuvenation and revitalization and a promotion of your health. When you have an autoimmune disease, you have to accommodate your new biological situation, and no one knows what the best physical activity plan is for you. But I think we can say, without a doubt, that daily movement is still critical for people with autoimmune diseases. Sitting motionless for hours each day is toxic for any person's body. Just remember that if you have not already talked with your healthcare provider about physical activity, you should plan to do so before you start making big changes in your movement or habits.

Make It Fun

The key to being physically active for life is enjoyment. A growing area of research in physical activity and wellness is the "Play" movement. Anytime you can make your physical activity something that makes you smile, appreciate, engage, and even be a little silly, you are much more likely to stick with it.

My dog knows how to make physical activity fun. She wakes up in the morning, takes a big stretch, lets out a yawn, and races for the door. She grabs a toy, teases me to try and catch her, and then races around the house with her prize. To her, this is not exercise, it is play. Playing is fun and she's not keeping score—although she does seem to take some satisfaction in the fact that I can't catch her.

Be sure that you mix at least some play into your physical activity plan—dance through the house to your favorite song, chase the dog around the yard, get a Hoola Hoop, or shoot a basketball. Move more and sit less.

The Space between the Notes

In every piece of music, the space between the notes is as important as the notes. Just as in music, it's important to put spaces of rest between your physical activities. Wellness requires that you cultivate the art of balance. As important as activity is, resting the body and the mind must also be a priority in order to be healthy. Resting can mean sleep, but it can also mean sitting quietly, taking some deep breaths, or watching the sun set.

Several years ago I attended a conference for researchers who were working in the areas of public health and parks and recreation. We were sharing our research and looking for areas where we could partner to promote health in the USA. One of the researchers from Parks and Recreation discussed a concept that had never occurred to me before, and it made me stop and think.

He discussed the non-physical-activity benefits of being in a park setting and pointed out that health and physical activity professionals tended to see parks only as a place to be physically active and burn calories. The Parks and

Recreation researchers, however, found important health benefits from just "being" in the park even when no physical activity was performed, including positive changes in blood pressure and stress hormones, to name just a couple. Just being outside in nature provides health benefits even when exercise doesn't occur.

Thinking about a visit to the park in this way made me feel as if I'd had a blind spot removed from my field of vision. What a liberating idea—you can go to the park and just sit on the bench, and it will be good for your health.

Healthy Eating

Healthy eating is more complicated than healthy physical activity. There are a lot of different opinions about what we should and should not eat. I believe in keeping things simple when it comes to diet, but I know some people might argue that I am doing myself a disservice by not exploring alternative-healing diet options. They could be right. I find it exhausting, though, to obsess over my diet.

I don't diet. I eat. I focus on a few reasonable habits and try to relax about the rest. I've taken many graduate courses in nutrition and have taught basic nutrition principles in my work. I think humans were designed to be able to work with a wide range of diets, and there is probably some biological "best fit" for each of us that is beyond what we know at this time.

A diet should be a guide rather than a mandate. You can get reliable and reasonable dietary guidance from health websites such as the Center for Disease Control and Prevention, (http://www.cdc.gov/HealthyLiving/), DASH (Dietary

Approaches to Stop Hypertension) (http://www.dashdiet. org/) and the American Dietetic Association (http://www. eatright.org/). A few simple habits to live by are: limit excess calories that provide little or no nutrition, limit sodium intake, limit processed food intake, eat fruits and vegetables daily, eat whole grains that have good levels of fiber (at least three grams per serving), drink enough water to have lightly colored urine, and eat healthy fats (plant fats, fish fats).

My body usually lets me know when I'm on the right track in terms of habitual eating. When I eat lower-fat and lower-sodium foods, I tend to feel better. When I limit meat intake, I tend to feel better. When I eat smaller portions, I tend to feel better. When I limit alcohol intake, I tend to feel better. When I get plenty of daily fiber, I tend to feel better. When I eat foods that are what I call "clean burning" (cause no burps, indigestion, or overfull feelings afterward), I tend to feel better. Occasionally eating junk is not a problem, but I know that consistently eating junk is careless and not in my best interest.

Scleroderma has made eating more challenging for me because of changes in my mouth, stomach, and intestines. You only need to experience a few "middle-of-the-night" projectile reflux incidents to quickly change the way you eat dinner in the future. Friends used to tease me for not ordering a meal if we were eating past eight o'clock or for turning down food if I thought I would have to stand for long periods of time after eating. Both of those scenarios created terrible stomach cramping and reflux for me shortly after-ward, and I found the avoidance of pain to be a powerful motivator. Initially my friends mistook my food or alcohol avoidance as an effort to control my weight and it might have annoyed them. Eventually, however, they accepted my habits and understood my circumstances. And frankly, I don't worry about what they think. I have to do what is best for me.

Likewise, you will have to find what works best for you. There is some research about foods that are thought to influence inflammation (either making it better or worse) but a lot of that science is still not well understood. It will be helpful to avoid foods that could make some of your symptoms worse such as alcohol, soft drinks, or acidic foods that promote dry mouth and cavities. Ideally you should find a registered dietitian who has experience with your particular condition and at least get feedback about your typical food choices and how they might interact with your disease or medications. Talking with other patients in a support group could also help you learn what works with your condition. Remember that you are still vulnerable to all of the health problems the general public is at risk for so try to eat foods that decrease your risk for heart disease, diabetes, and cancer.

Let's Talk about Weight

Both Linda and I have experienced weight changes as a result of our diseases. I have experienced relentless swelling in my lower legs, feet, and hands as well as bloating and sluggish intestines that can change my waistline from day to day. Linda has had to deal with weight gain as great as twenty-five pounds as a result of steroid medications. Regardless of the cause, weight gain can place a strain on your physical and emotional health. Excess weight places an additional burden on your heart and endocrine system, which compounds the damage caused by an autoimmune disease. In addition, it is one more alteration of your physical self and your identity that you have to endure. Keeping a healthy weight not only helps you to minimize some of the negative physical impact of your autoimmune disease, it can also help you feel better about yourself in the face of all the other changes you are going through.

Lupus and scleroderma don't necessarily result in weight gain. Sometimes people with these diseases can experience losing too much muscle tissue or being under-weight. I am always struck by how many women in our scleroderma support group are extremely thin. Being under-weight is as much of a health problem as being overweight. Getting a healthy amount of physical activity and establishing a healthy eating routine can promote the maintenance of muscle and limit the amount of stored fat—important investments in your overall health.

We all have to move our *buts*—those handy excuses we're all so good at creating—so we can optimize our health within the constraints of our diseases. We no longer have the luxury to overtax our physical health without paying a high price. Be gentle but firm with yourself. Add movement to your daily life, invest in a healthy diet, get the rest you need, and have some fun. Your habits don't have to be perfect but try to make them consistent. Even doing each of these a little better today than you did yester-day will improve your wellbeing.

Sadness

By Karen

I am still surprised at how quickly I can
tumble down into that dark place.
It starts as a step back. Then another, and another.
And suddenly I am tumbling down.
And as I drop down I pass each thought
that helped to push me down here.

Blue Dawn

By Karen

Blue dawn marks the start of another day,
A deep, blue jewel that fades into white.
In the quiet of the blue dawn light,
Life begins to stir with the morning
songs of the birds and dogs.
Each morning, I share in the fleeting,
mystical transformation.
As the deep blue sky is drained away,
It serves as evidence of the earth's constant movement,
Evidence of our temporariness.
No matter how beautiful or majestic,
In this blue dawn we cannot stay long.

Prayer

By Karen

Dear Lord,
Help me to fill my life with beauty.
Help me to feel love and to be buffered against hate.
I know I can't walk a stress-free path, but help
me to lighten the burden of nonsense.

Afterword

Metamorphosis

By Karen

OR ME, THE ugly dress started out as a symbol for how I felt about scleroderma. It also symbolized how I felt about myself. I think I was initially trying to inject a little humor into my situation with scleroderma. It wasn't until Linda and I were well into writing the book that I connected an early childhood memory with my choice to call scleroderma my ugly dress.

When I was a preschooler, my family lived in rural Pennsylvania close to our extended family. My paternal grandfather had a farm-like setup on his land, and at one point he brought a small herd of young sheep to the property and said that each of the lambs "belonged" to one of the grandchildren. We each had to name our lamb. The lamb that was assigned to me was the only dark-colored sheep in the herd. I remember my family wanted to call my lamb "Ugly" because she was different from the others. They thought it was a funny name. I thought it was mean to give her the name Ugly and would hurt her feelings. I didn't want to call her Ugly.

My family's humor prevailed and my lamb was named Ugly. Of course the lamb did not care but I did get the message. Ugly was anything that did not conform to some standard. Ugly was to be made fun of; ugly was inferior. My lamb could have been named so many other things that reflected her uniqueness, her specialness and beauty. Her label, however, reflected the opinion of others, not the truth about herself.

My initial labeling of scleroderma as my "ugly dress" reflected my feelings and fears. But working with Linda to write this book helped me to re-examine my feelings. Ugly is just a word, a "growl" word that reflects my feelings about my experience but does not reflect who I am. I loved my lamb and she was never ugly to me. I also love my life and, in spite of scleroderma, I am not ugly either. While I cannot control what outside opinions might be about scleroderma or scleroderma's effects on me, I can control my opinion about my life, my dress. And I know that my life is as beautiful as all the rest. Through the process of "accessorizing" with Linda, I am allowing a metamorphosis of my life with scleroderma into something quite beautiful despite having to wear an "ugly dress."

Afterword

It's Time!

By Linda

I LOVE BEING WITH my great nieces and nephews. Their childish *joie de vivre* is contagious, and when I take time to listen to them, I am continuously delighted and enlightened by the things they say.

One beautiful spring day, I was outside watching about five of my "greats" romping and playing in my niece's yard. Four-year-old Mitchell had just come from kindergarten and his dad said, "Mitchell, show Aunt Linda what happened to you today." Mitchell obediently pulled up his trouser leg to show me where he had fallen and scraped his shin. Of course, the area was protectively covered by a Spider Man

Band-Aid so I couldn't really tell the extent of the injury, but I knew my duty as an aunt and "oohed" and "aahed" appropriately. I noticed that in addition to the Band-Aided injury, his leg had numerous little bruises and scars where he had previously injured himself. I remarked on these as well. Mitchell called over his shoulder as he ran to play, "I'm just a broken little boy, Aunt Linda."

After my diagnosis of lupus and the trauma of divorce, I too felt broken. My scars weren't visible like Mitchell's, but they were there all the same. Learning that you have a serious chronic illness and that (oh, by the way) the man you've been married to your entire adult life is leaving, is like being hit by an eighteen-wheeler. If you survive the hit—and it's a big *if*—you look very carefully before crossing a road again.

I found my broken self to be very distrustful. I was distrustful of my ability to make good decisions, and I was especially distrustful of men. If my husband had left me because of the lupus, how could I expect anyone else to be attracted to me, let alone stay with me? Besides, how could I trust another man? After all, nothing had really changed. I was still me and I still had lupus.

It was a year before I took even tentative tippy-toe steps toward dating again. One evening while at dinner with two of my closest friends, I mentioned that it might be enjoyable to go to dinner or a movie occasionally with a nice man— nothing serious, just a casual outing now and then. That conversation was all it took for Jane, the matchmaker of our group, to swing into action.

In less than a week she called and said she had someone

she wanted me to meet. She had already talked with him and said he would like to call but would not do so without my permission. "By the way," she added casually, "he's eight years younger than you and he's never been married. Also, he just broke up with someone and he's devastated!"

Not exactly a sales pitch, but how could any of that matter? It was just a casual get-together, right?

He called that evening and we arranged to meet. He told me later that he was expecting to meet at some public place so that either of us could escape easily if the meeting didn't go well. I, however, was not up on all the dating rules. During my nearly three decades of marriage, the world and dating etiquette had changed significantly. I never liked the games of dating when I was young, and I had no intention of playing them now. I knew that I was not about to sit anxiously in a restaurant or some other public place wearing a carnation in my lapel or holding a rose in my teeth so that I could be easily recognized and easily rejected without even knowing the blind date had come and gone. Instead, I asked him over to my house for Sunday dinner.

On Sunday evening, I opened the door and greeted my future husband, although obviously neither of us knew it at the time. We talked for hours that first night. I told him about the lupus because if he was going to run, I wanted him to do it sooner rather than later. He asked if I had anything to read that would help him understand lupus better. He told me that his father had been a doctor and that he had actually started college thinking he wanted to be a doctor as well. I think the chemistry courses changed his mind.

The next time we got together, he had not only read the

material on lupus but asked me lots of questions. This could not have been more unlike my ex-husband's response to my illness.

From then on, Will and I started to date regularly—every Wednesday and Saturday for several months and then more often. Soon he was at my house more than his own, and when we weren't together we were on the telephone. I felt a strong connection to Will, but I still had a lot of issues to overcome. There were numerous emotional triggers from my previous relationship, including my insecurity about my femininity and desirability. After all, I had been dumped! I was extremely defensive and reactive to anything remotely critical during this early phase of the relationship, taking everything much too personally.

I was also very protective of the new home I'd made for myself. Instead of having to compromise or bow to my ex-husband's taste, I had made my new home entirely a reflection of me. My son summed it up when he visited for the first time, remarking to one of my friends, "I just love Mom's new home. It's so-o-o Mom!" I had created a sanctuary of tranquility and beauty. The intrusion of a man, other than my son, into my space was difficult at first.

When you add lupus and steroids to the emotional chaos of divorce, I was a mess. It took a lot of time and a lot of work to build a trusting relationship with Will. Fortunately for me he was patient, and we both believed the relationship was worth the work. During the eight years we dated—yes, I said eight—we journeyed through happy times, not so happy times, and tragic times. We celebrated joyful occasions with extended family and friends. We helped each other through devastating losses (my brother, his sister, my precious great-niece). He supported me and cared for me through numerous lupus flares and one hospitalization. Through it all, we learned and grew as a couple.

On December 23, 2005, I invited Will's brothers and their families over for our traditional Christmas gathering. His nieces (ages eleven and five) and nephew (age eight) spent the afternoon with me baking Christmas cookies and preparing dinner for everyone. By the end of the evening when everyone gathered in the living room for dessert, I was totally exhausted.

Will waited for everyone to settle down with their desserts and then said, "I want to tell ya'll a story about Linda. You know how tired she gets with the lupus, and you know that she has to get up very early during the week to drive to Clemson. So you would think that on weekends, she would stay in bed most of the day. Not so! She always gets up around eight or nine o'clock. 'Why are you getting up so early?' I ask nearly every time. Now Linda, tell them what you *always* say in reply."

Not having a clue where he was going, I repeated my usual response: "It's time."

He smiled broadly and said, "Honey, you're right. It's time!" Then he stood, pulled out a ring box, and got on his knees in front of me.

Before he actually asked the question or I could respond, the room erupted with excitement. Keelin, Will's eleven-year-old niece, jumped over the coffee table, landing in my lap and knocking over her mother's coffee in the process. His brothers sat with mouths agape. Had they really just witnessed their fifty-three-year-old bachelor brother proposing marriage?

We assume that somewhere in the middle of the chaos, Will actually asked the question and I responded. Who knows? At any rate, we got married six months later, and we are thankful each day for the blessing of being together.

Will's theme of "It's time!" also played out in relation to my work. I had struggled for twelve years to keep working in spite of the lupus. Many times over the years, I came close to giving up. Each time, I followed my own and Karen's advice about accessorizing: pause, assess, and then choose. I always fully utilized the pause. What I found worked well for me was to define a specific deadline: "If I'm not better at the end of December, I'll stop working." Usually, by the time the deadline arrived I did feel better, so I'd keep going until the next time.

I also tried other things in order to keep working. During one prolonged flare, I volunteered to participate in the first phase of a clinical trial for epratuzumab, a monoclonal antibody that is under development as a potential new treatment for lupus. The first phase of a drug trial tests the safety and effectiveness of the drug in humans. I believe strongly in the value of clinical research because I know how important it is to continue to develop new treatments for lupus and other diseases. New drugs can't get to market unless they're tested thoroughly with human volunteers.

In this case, I rationalized that even if the drug didn't help me, it might help someone else. The treatments did help for awhile and allowed me to keep working about nine months longer. I would have continued them but when phase I of the research study ended, there was a delay in availability of the drug due to a manufacturing issue.

I had asked my doctor many times over the years, "How can I know for certain that it's time to stop working?"

His reply was always, "I never push my patients to stop but I'll support you when you get to that point. You'll know when it's time." He was right. I realized that I could no longer do my job the way I knew it needed to be done. I knew my staff deserved the very best leadership, so I finally let go.

Thomas Paine said that if we obtain something too easily, we esteem it too lightly and that *dearness only* gives everything its value. I will say that my present happiness and contentment were dearly won. Flannery O'Connor described illness as a journey, and it has certainly been one for me. I would not wish lupus or other serious illness on anyone. Trust me—there are easier ways to learn life's lessons. However, because lupus slowed me down, at times to a complete standstill, it forced me to really examine myself and how I wanted to live my life.

People respond in different ways to serious illnesses or other life crises. At the beginning of my journey, I vowed that I would get through it with grace and dignity. I chose to use my illness and the divorce as opportunities to learn and grow. Someone once told me that you cannot grow and mature until you are able to mentally stand yourself in a corner and objectively examine your actions. You can't judge yourself simply by your good intentions. What choices do you make? What actions do you take?

Change is inevitable. We will all experience illness, loss of loved ones, and other challenges at some point in our lives, but we can always choose how we respond. Maturity involves continuously examining ourselves and continuously changing and growing. As T. S. Eliot said, "We must not cease from exploration and the end of all our exploring will be to arrive where we began and to know the place for the first time."

Ugly Dress Revisited

By Linda

The ugly dress I thought I'd despise
Changed my heart and opened my eyes.
I lived my life in a frenzied pace,
Not pausing to think, "Life's not a race."
Lupus said, "Halt," and against my will,
I learned life's lesson: "Peace. Be still."

About the Authors

Linda McNamara, RN, MBA

Linda is a registered nurse, healthcare consultant, and certified health coach with over forty years experience in health and wellness. She has been living with systemic lupus since 1996.

Karen A. Kemper, PhD, MSPH

Karen is a health educator and university professor in health promotion and public health. She has certifications in health fitness and life coaching and has worked in health and wellness for twenty-five years. She has been living with scleroderma since 1992.

Acknowledgements

Linda

I EXTEND MY DEEPEST love and appreciation to all the "yellow buoys" and "helicopters" in my life. You're always there for me when life gets rough and give me something to hold on to until I can gather strength and move on. On occasion, you've even lifted me out of danger and provided me with a safe place to heal. I am filled with thanksgiving that you are in my life:

- My husband: William Fewell McNamara
- My son: Phillip Randolph Crew
- My mother: Opal Reeves
- My sisters: Faye Bryan, Barbara Franklin, Janice Grissett, and Tracee Nix

- My dear friends: Linda Morgan, Linda Marlowe, Jane Garner, Karen Kemper, Charlotte Rigby, Suzanne Fortin, Janet Bauer, Robbie Hughes, and Wanda Moore.

A special thank you to those who read our first bungling attempts at a coherent manuscript: Jane Garner, Linda Marlowe, Charlotte Rigby, Dava Sobel, Amye Leong, Gina Turcotte, Heather Windsor, and Janet Bauer; and to Mary Anne Maier, editor extraordinaire. Your encouragement kept us going and your insights and constructive criticism helped us immensely. Finally, I extend my heartfelt appreciation to the wonderful and talented individuals at the Joseph F. Sullivan Center, Clemson University and Interim Healthcare, Greenville, South Carolina. It has been my honor and privilege to work with such caring and competent people.

Acknowledgements

Karen

$\mathcal{I}$ AM VERY GRATEFUL to my friends, family, and healers who have helped me have the strength to share my experience of the ugly dress. I have been shy about sharing so many thoughts and feelings about living with scleroderma. While I was very comfortable writing about my experiences, I learned that I was not as comfortable with other people reading what I wrote. I have wanted to be honest about my experience but have worried about hurting the people I love with my frustration, fear, and pain. It is the friendship and love of these people, however, which ultimately made this book possible. I cannot thank them all but I want to acknowledge several here. First, I want to thank my dear friend, Linda McNamara, whose strength and courage made this book a reality. I also want to thank my mother, Patricia Kemper, and my father, Richard Kemper, for raising me to be a strong and independent person who could weather the storm of scleroderma and still have a beautiful life. Another person who has had a tremendous influence on who I am today is Kathy Murtiashaw. She planted the seed of desire to write a book (Yeah, do it!). I am also very grateful to Gail Virardi and Dianne Greyerbiehl who have helped me heal personally and spiritually. I am immensely grateful to Dr. Marcy Bolster and Toni Masters for their ongoing compassionate care of my physical wellbeing that has allowed me to live so well. And finally, I want to thank my "Greenville Circle of Friends" buddies. They are one of my most precious "accessories," and their friendship is invaluable to me.

References

- Allen, Donna, Deb Carlson and 'Chelle Ham (2007). "Well-Being: New Paradigms of Wellness—Inspiring Positive Health Outcomes and Renewing Hope." *American Journal of Health Promotion.* Jan/Feb.
- Breslow, Lester (2006). "Health: Measurement in the third era of public health." *American Journal of Public Health.* 96:17–19.
- Butler, Gillian and Tony Hope (2007). *Managing Your Mind: The Mental Fitness Guide.* Second edition. Oxford University Press. Oxford, New York.
- Durstine, Larry and Geoffrey Moore (2003). *ACSM's Exercise Management for Persons with Chronic Disease and Disabilities.* 2nd edition. Human Kinetics, Champaign, Illinois.

- Dyer, Wayne W. (2007). *Change Your Thoughts — Change Your Life.* Hay House, Inc., p 189.
- Fisher, Bruce and Robert Alberti (2000). *Rebuilding When Your Relationship Ends.* Third edition. Impact Publishers, Inc. Atascadero, California.
- Gibran, Kahlil. (1923). *The Prophet.* Ninety-fourth printing. Alfred A. Knopf, Inc., New York, New York. p 52.
- Housden, Roger (2001). *Ten Poems to Change Your Life.* Harmony Books. New York, New York. p 43.
- Kabat-Zinn, Jon (1990). *Full Catastrophe Living: Using the Wisdom of Your Body and Mind to Face Stress, Pain and Illness.* Dell Publishing, New York, New York.
- Lindbergh, Anne Morrow *(1955, 1975). Gift from the Sea.* Pantheon Books, New York, New York. pp 113–115.
- Myss, Caroline (1997). *Why People Don't Heal and How They Can.* Three Rivers Press. New York, New York. pp 13–15.
- National Center for Complementary and Alternative Medicine. National Institutes of Health. *Backgrounder.* "Energy Medicine: An Overview." [On-line]. Available: http://www.nccam.nih.gov. Accessed 7/5/09.
- National Center for Complementary and Alternative Medicine. National Institutes of Health. CAM Overview. [On-line]. Available: http://www.nccam.nih.gov. Accessed 8/5/09.
- National Institute of Neurological Disorders and Stroke Brain Basics, Understanding Sleep. [On-line]. Available: http://www.ninds.nih.gov/. Accessed 8/5/09.
- National Institute of Mental Health, National Institutes

of Health. "Psychotherapies." [On-line]. Available: http://www.nimh.gov. Accessed July, 2009.

- Office of Women's Health. Department of Health and Human Services. "Autoimmune Diseases." [On-line]. Available: http://www.4woman.gov. Accessed 3/21/00.
- Remen, Rachel Naomi (1994). *Kitchen Table Wisdom.* Riverhead Books. New York, New York. p 217.
- Reilly & Lee Publishers. (1958). *One Hundred and One Famous Poems.* An anthology compiled by Cook, Roy J. p 135.
- Urban, Hal. (2004). *Positive Words, Powerful Results.* Fireside, Rockefeller Center. New York, New York. pp 44–45.
- Viscott, David (1996). *Emotional Resilience: Simple Truths for Dealing with the Unfinished Business of Your Past.* Three Rivers Press. New York, New York.
- Whitfield, Charles L. (1993). *Boundaries and Relationships: Knowing, Protecting and Enjoying the Self.* Health Communications, Inc., Deerfield Beach, Florida.